€ 4 -
ART
22/1

ENCOMPASSING BRITAIN

PAINTING AT THE POINTS OF THE COMPASS

ENCOMPASSING BRITAIN

PAINTING AT THE POINTS OF THE COMPASS

Peter Collyer

THOMAS REED PUBLICATIONS

A DIVISION OF THE ABR COMPANY LIMITED

I dedicate this to the men and women
who crew our fishing fleet.

"The real price of fish is the lives of men."

The above quotation is taken from a memorial to lost Fleetwood-based trawlers.

Published by
Thomas Reed Publications
(a division of The ABR Company Limited)
The Barn, Ford Farm
Bradford Leigh, Bradford on Avon
Wiltshire BA15 2RP
United Kingdom

First published in Great Britain 2002

British Library Cataloguing in Publication Data
A CIP catalogue record for this book is available from the
British Library

Edited by John Lloyd
Design and page layout by Eric Drewery
Printed in China by Compass Press Limited

ISBN 1 904050 02 6

Peter Collyer is represented by
Chris Beetles Ltd, St James's, London
Telephone 020 7839 7551
Specialists in English Watercolours
www.chrisbeetles.com
www.petercollyer.co.uk

CONTENTS

FOREWORD

by Libby Purves

When you sail round Britain and Ireland you feel a gradually building sense of wonder. These little islands off the great wedge of Europe seem to get bigger, not smaller, by virtue of their variety. The coastline, rather than being homogenized by the presence of the sea, is startlingly diverse in its scenery, shapes and smells – high, low, rocky, grassy, muddy, sandy, bleak or lush in turn. Birds and seals haunt the shoreline; the sea itself is infinitely variable, from pond-smooth to gently ruffled or high and wild, smashing against the rocks.

Gradually, as the voyage progresses, you also come to feel a sense of ownership. There is something very satisfying about living on an island and being able to go all round it, or (if you are on a boat) to approach it from any angle or point of the compass you choose. And when without a boat you walk one of the many coastal paths, usually maintained by the National Trust's Neptune Coastline Campaign, you get a parallel satisfaction: measuring the shape of the coast step by slithering step in all its rugged or marshy illogicality, a kind of daft pride grows in you as if you had built it all yourself. I suspect that Peter Collyer's book will have a similar effect.

Those who loved his *Rain Later, Good*, profiling the Shipping Forecast areas, or his later book *South by Southwest*, will know that he is not only a marvellous, delicate draughtsman and watercolourist (who appears willing to work in the most revolting weather conditions) but a dryly observant writer and a knowledgeable amateur naturalist. To chronicle the sea-coast appears to be his chosen life's work, and we should be grateful. The device of using points of the compass is calculated to appeal to all traditionalist maritime sensibilities, even if it does turn out rather disconcertingly that the centre of the British island universe is only 20 kilometres from the Lancashire coast. Altogether, this book is an eccentric enterprise, and a laborious one, and all the better for that. I suspect it will inspire many pilgrimages.

INTRODUCTION

"How about doing the points of the compass?" It was Allan Brunton-Reed speaking.

I was intrigued, if at first a little puzzled.

"Points of the compass?"

"You could visit the last landfall in Britain at the 32 points of the compass. We could get Harry Baker to calculate them for you."

Harry Baker is an expert on navigation and produces an annually updated book about navigating at sea by the stars, *Reed's Heavenly Bodies.* Go to the Reed's Nautical Books stand at the Boat Show and you will find it on the top shelf along with Playbuoy.

"We would have to find a suitable starting point for him to calculate from, presumably it would have to be the geographical centre of Britain, wherever that is."

Somewhere near Birmingham is the most common response I get. Someone who thinks they know might suggest Meriden, a village between Solihull and Coventry. It sounds like meridian. This ought to be the line running through the centre of the country, but it isn't. Slice off everything east of the meridian and we would only lose East Anglia, Kent, East Sussex, a bit of Lincolnshire and Spurn Head.

Those often suggested central points are close to that of England alone – if you can wait a moment while I put my anorak on – which is actually off the A5 just north of Nuneaton.

I suspected the centre of Britain would be somewhere further north, we folk down south forget just how big the land of the wee folk up north really is. To get a definitive answer to where the centre is I spoke to a very helpful man at the Ordnance Survey in Southampton.

I was given three alternatives from which to choose. The centre of the mainland only, the mainland plus the seven major islands (which are Anglesey, Arran, Islay, Isle of Wight, Jura, Mull, and Skye – I knew you would want to know that) or the mainland with 401 associated islands. Of course none of these options included Northern Ireland, which is part of the United Kingdom but not Great Britain and has its own Ordnance Survey, or the Isle of Man and the Channel Islands, which are Crown Dependencies, not part of Britain at all, just nearby.

I decided that the most comprehensive option to go for was the one that included the 401 islands, although 'mainland' Britain has 6,289 islands in all.

How do you calculate the centre of Britain?

Well, to cut a long story short, back in the 1960s when the Ordnance Survey first set a team to work on it, they basically pasted a large map of the country on to a board and stuck a pin in the underside to find out the point at which it balanced. That's true, honest. There is a mathematical formula for calculating the centre of an irregular shape and a computer

will calculate the point in moments. Strangely, the pin and computer methods produced, give or take a few hundred metres, the same result.

So here it is: the centre of Britain as far as the Ordnance Survey people are concerned is at 54°0.2'N 2°33.3'W. Using OS grid references, that is SD 637 565. On the ground it is four miles north-west of the village of Dunsop Bridge in the Forest of Bowland, near Clitheroe in Lancashire: a mere 12 miles from the Lancashire coast near Morecambe to the west and 96 miles from the Yorkshire coast near Bridlington to the east.

Can I take my anorak off now?

Those of you who were Scouts or Guides or who survived school geography lessons will, I hope, remember that the compass is more than simply north, east, south and west. There are named points in between; a puzzle to some, but vital to those who want to get somewhere in life.

What happens when you place a compass onto a map of Britain and draw a line in each of the 32 directions radiating from the centre? As the lines reach the coast, crossing the last piece of Britain's land we are given 32 points, every one equally separated from its neighbour by 11.25°, and also curiously united with the other 31 points by that same even spacing around the compass.

Britain's coast of course does not encompass a perfect circle of land. In its 7,000 or so miles there are small bays and headlands, peninsulas, estuaries ... and all those islands. Consequently the 32 points are not evenly placed around our coastline. For instance, in Lancashire west-south-west and west-by-south are only eight miles apart, yet there is not one single point on the entire east coast of Scotland.

I was intrigued to see what Harry Baker's calculations would give me. What 32 arbitrarily selected places would be occupying my thoughts during the two years I would have to travel, paint and write myself around them? Where are they? How much variety of landscape would I encounter? What if half of them are mud flats or chemical works? Would I be making any return trips to familiar territory? Will there be anywhere totally inaccessible? Will there be lots of good fish to eat?

Before I visited any of the 32 coastal points I needed first to travel to the central spot, to begin at the beginning ...

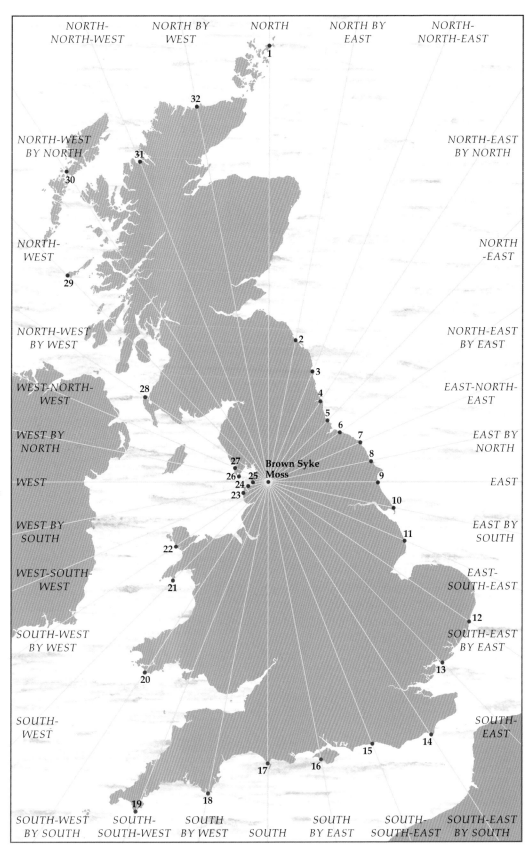

NORTH-
NORTH-WEST

NORTH BY
WEST

NORTH

NORTH BY
EAST

NORTH-
NORTH-EAST

32 Farr, Highland

31 Badluarach,
Highland

30 Sgarasta Bheag,
South Harris,
Western Isles

29 Cornaig, Tiree,
Argyll & Bute

28 Corsewall Point,
Dumfries &
Galloway

27 Duddon Sands,
Cumbria

26 Isle of Walney,
Cumbria

25 Sunderland
Point,
Lancashire

24 Pilling Marsh,
Lancashire

23 Cleveleys,
Lancashire

22 Rhosneigr,
Isle of Anglesey

21 Porth Neigwl,
Gwynedd

20 West Pickard Bay,
Pembrokeshire

19 Loe Bar,
Cornwall

18 Bolt Head,
Devon

17 Chesil Bank,
Dorset

NORTH-WEST
BY NORTH

NORTH-
WEST

NORTH-WEST
BY WEST

WEST-NORTH-
WEST

WEST BY
NORTH

WEST

WEST BY
SOUTH

WEST-SOUTH-
WEST

SOUTH-WEST
BY WEST

SOUTH-
WEST

SOUTH-WEST
BY SOUTH

SOUTH-
SOUTH-WEST

SOUTH
BY WEST

SOUTH

SOUTH
BY EAST

SOUTH-
SOUTH-EAST

SOUTH-EAST
BY SOUTH

SOUTH-EAST
BY EAST

SOUTH-
EAST

EAST-
SOUTH-EAST

EAST BY
SOUTH

EAST

EAST BY
NORTH

EAST-NORTH-
EAST

NORTH-EAST
BY EAST

NORTH
-EAST

NORTH-EAST
BY NORTH

Brown Syke
Moss

1 Whitemill Bay,
Sanday, Orkney
Islands

2 Berwick-upon-
Tweed,
Northumberland

3 Boulmer,
Northumberland

4 Tynemouth,
Tyne & Wear

5 Horden,
County Durham

6 Coatham, Redcar,
Redcar &
Cleveland

7 Whitby,
North Yorkshire

8 Scalby Ness,
Scarborough,
North Yorkshire

9 Ulrome &
Skipsea,
East Riding of
Yorkshire

10 Waxholme,
Withernsea,
East Riding of
Yorkshire

11 North End,
Mablethorpe,
Lincolnshire

12 Southwold,
Suffolk

13 Clacton-on-Sea,
Essex

14 Dungeness,
Kent

15 Goring-by-Sea,
West Sussex

16 Tennyson Down,
Isle of Wight

FINDING THE CENTRE

BROWN SYKE MOSS, FOREST OF BOWLAND
LANCASHIRE

The hub of Dunsop Bridge village is an old humpback bridge over a wide, shallow, fast-flowing river with a rock-strewn bed, unsurprisingly named the River Dunsop. Between the road and the river is the small village green, overlooked by magnificent trees and populated by ducks and wagtails.

Opposite the green stands the Post Office where visitors can buy a map giving directions for the seven and a half mile (that's there and back) 'Centre of Britain Walk'. I quizzed the postmistress about the walk only to find to my surprise that she had not attempted it. How can you live so close to somewhere like that and not go there? I'm sure everyone living within four miles of Land's End or John O'Groats must have been to their respective landmarks. I know I would be overcome with inquisitiveness.

I stayed overnight on the edge of the village at Wood End Farm which, I discovered from the tenants, was part of the Duchy of Lancaster Estate. Since the reign of Henry IV the title 'Duke of Lancaster' has been held by the monarch, so the present Duke is the Queen.

That would explain 'Forest' in the area's name, used in this case in the traditional sense of a royal hunting ground. Wild boar, deer and wolves once roamed here. Now it is sheep, cattle and the occasional walker.

The Queen came to the farm once, not to stay for B&B as I had, just for a look round as a neighbour might do. Perhaps she popped in to borrow a cup of sugar. Apparently this area is one of her favourite places.

A thought crossed my mind that the exact centre of Britain might actually belong to the Queen as the Duke. How appropriate that would be. Alas, I discovered that this is not the case. A company going by the rather dull and anonymous name of United Utilities has that honour. How sad!

The first half of the walk from Dunsop Bridge to the centre is a gentle, level stroll along a well made track through a narrow valley beside the River Dunsop, with plantations of conifers on the hillsides

54°0.2'N 2°33.3'W

and horned sheep with their maturing lambs grazing the verges.

Aware that these were my first steps along a journey that would eventually take me to all points round the kingdom's shores, it seemed a little strange to be starting with an inland walk, but I could not have begun anywhere else. I needed to find out what the centre looks like, to discover what is there. On my journey round the coast I would no doubt have to explain many times what these travels were about, so how could I answer the question 'What is at the centre of Britain?' with 'I don't know, I haven't been there yet'.

What a shame the centre is not Duchy of Lancaster land. It is the second Duke, John of Gaunt who makes the 'this scept'red isle … this precious stone set in a silver sea' speech in Shakespeare's *Richard II*. How fitting that would have been. At least my walk to the centre started out from Duchy land, so perhaps it is in order to quote a little more: 'This fortress built by nature for herself … bound in with the triumphant sea, whose rocky shore beats back the envious siege of wat'ry Neptune'.

I'd be witnessing plenty of that along the way, that was for sure.

At about the half-way point the track passes through a water pumping station and continues on to a group of farm buildings, after which the route becomes more difficult. After an exhausting climb over a steep fell I found myself gazing out across an area of rolling peat moorland thick with heather. If only I had come in August when the heather is in bloom I would have found myself, as the Bard might have said 'a tired twelve-stone set in a purple sea'.

Surrounding me at about three to four miles distance was a series of hills a little higher than my vantage point at about 500 metres. In my immediate vicinity millions of heads of cotton grass nodded in the breeze. At my feet … well they were slowly disappearing as I sank slowly into the peat. I soon learned not to stand still for too long.

Walking across this proved a little tricky. Springy under foot, some places were more boggy than others and until I had put my foot down it was impossible to tell just how far I would sink before I could take the next step.

The peat was cut through by what appeared to be a series of dry ponds and river beds about a metre deep and several metres across showing smooth, peat-black, rounded gullies and bowls.

I found this a little puzzling. Here I stood, 500 metres high on fairly level ground which sloped gently away in every direction, staring into empty watercourses which at some time or other must flow with considerable amounts of water in order to cut such well defined channels.

Where does all that water come from?

Two months later I found the answer. On a BBC Radio 4 weather forecast Helen Young announced that 54 millimetres of rain fell in the Forest of Bowland in one hour.

The next day I checked this with the Met. Office and was told it was a realistic figure for the area.

Fortunately I had an almost cloudless June sky as I squelched the final steps to my target. The journey from Dunsop Bridge had taken two hours. I had made it to this modest moorland hillside and felt that my travels to encompass Britain really had begun.

The unmarked centre sits on a south-west facing hillside known as Brown Syke Moss. Two watercourses, Brown Syke and Round Hill Water flow

down the hillside with the centre on a spur of land between them, just upstream from their confluence.

I was pleased that the centre was somewhere remote but accessible, wild and silent like this and not in a ghastly shopping mall or by the side of a noisy dual carriageway. It seemed appropriate as this was how many of us like to think of our country, a timeless vision of Albion, a rural idyll, with nothing but the breeze, a view of distant hills and not a building in sight.

It might be the centre of the land mass of Britain but this blessed plot is all about water. I spoke to

United Utilities men on the spot (well actually they – the Estate Manager and the Wildlife Officer – were in their Bowland Estate Office in the nearby village of Slaidburn) to find out what they own and why.

United Utilities, formerly known as North West Water, own more than 9,700 hectares (about 37.5 square miles) of the Forest of Bowland. The land is a catchment area for rainwater and their ownership ensures they have control over the land's use in order to keep the catchment clean, being much better for them (and us as consumers) than trying to clean it later on in the process.

dry water course through the heather

There are heavy restraints on what farmers are allowed to put on the land, even if it's only the organic matter that farm animals produce naturally.

I only encountered a few sheep on the lower slopes, but was informed that the higher heather-covered moor is also grazed all year round by a flock of 600 to 700 ewes. The heather is a good food source for them and is burned on a rotation basis, revitalising the plants and providing the sheep with a regular supply of young shoots which are more nutritious.

The burning process is a winter activity that has to be carried out when the ground is moist in order to ensure that fires do not get out of control. None is allowed after April 15th to protect the habitats of ground nesting birds. The fells are an important site for golden plover, red grouse, curlew and meadow pipit.

At the farm near to the pumping station I encountered a pair of vociferous (aren't they always?) oystercatchers a long way from their natural environment. These are a particular favourite of mine, their call a sound I always associate with being at the coast, after all you find seagulls almost anywhere now. I took this as a symbol of the journeys that lay ahead of me, as if they were saying, 'We'll be catching up with you later'.

United Utilities have an open access policy, although there are no signs indicating the route to the centre and after the pumping station most walkers take a different path that leads to the scenic walk round one of their reservoirs.

"Do you get many people doing the walk to the centre like I have?" I asked.

The long pause before the reply of "Not really" somehow gave me the impression that they were wondering whether to supplement their answer with "you're the first one daft enough to try it".

Brennand Farm Oystercatcher

NORTH TO EAST

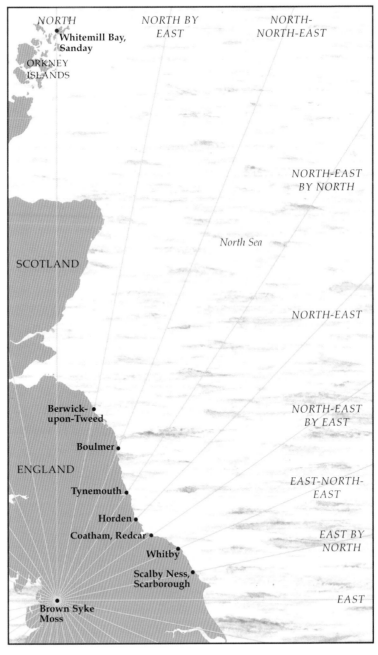

NORTH

WHITEMILL BAY
SANDAY, ORKNEY ISLANDS

When I first saw the map showing the 32 places I would be visiting, I had a feeling that this was going to be the most difficult one to get to.

I prefer to build a certain amount of flexibility into a painting trip to allow for the vagaries of our great British climate, traffic, and the time it could take to find a suitable subject once I'm there. I have some idea of where I might be from day to day, but usually book somewhere to stay for the first night only and take it from there. However, some locations present more of a problem. This was going to be less a trip, more an expedition and would need planning with military precision.

I could have flown to Sanday via Edinburgh and Kirkwall, but chose to drive to experience the many changes, both topographical and cultural, that occur as one crosses Britain from south to north. I knew that I could reach Stirling comfortably in a day, a mere 420 miles from home, but north of there I was a little unsure until I had studied the road atlas and the ferry timetables.

Just the thought of going to Scotland again brought a tingle of excitement.

Ferries to Orkney run overnight from Aberdeen, or in a mere two hours from the north coast near Thurso. I opted for the latter. Once there I would need to catch a second ferry to take me on to Sanday. With the first ferry sailings at 6am and then midday there was no prospect of catching one on the second day of my journey, so I had a more leisurely drive across the Highlands, with time to enjoy them looking glorious in their late autumn colours.

I had decided to stay the second night in Wick and catch the midday ferry the following day, but mis-timed the journey arriving there at 2.30pm, more than two hours earlier than expected. It's not that often I find myself with free time, but with John O'Groats only 17 miles away there was time to take a trip out there. Although it's not on my list of must-see places, I could not come all this way and miss it, at least I could say 'been there'.

What a grim place it is; a car park with shops, but a great view of Orkney. Sorry John O'Groats, I love everything about Scotland (a rash statement, I know), but here I'll make an exception. I cannot imagine how it can be the furthest place from Lands End when Duncansby Head (now there's somewhere that goes off the wow factor scale; 'been there') is another two miles to the east.

On day three's first ferry (that's the one that runs

59°18.2'N 2°32.5'W

from Scrabster on the island most of us call the mainland to Stromness on the island Orcadians call Mainland) I met a couple from Yorkshire who were 'emigrating' to Sanday's neighbouring island Westray. They had visited it for the first time eight months before, fallen in love with it, gone back to Yorkshire to put their house on the market and give up their jobs and now they were bringing out a JCB to start building their new home.

It gets you like that out here.

After arriving in Stromness I drove the 15 miles across Mainland to the outer islands ferry terminal at Kirkwall to catch the evening sailing to Sanday. Orkney Ferries please note: When you replace your fleet, consider placing windows where those of us who would like to take in the scenery can actually look out of them. Having to kneel on the seat for a view is not the best way of showing off what you have.

I finally arrived at 6pm after three days of travelling. Seven hundred and fifty miles and four hours afloat gave a good sense of Sanday's geographical isolation.

With the exception of a couple of low hills in the south-west, the island is a sandy reef in the form of three low peninsulas branching out from the centre to link a number of rocky outcrops. Thirteen miles from end to end, all the bays and headlands create a coastline that is more than 80 miles long.

Most of the island is a tree-less landscape of fertile farmland with fields bounded by yellow lichen covered dry-stone walls. With nothing to get in the way there are distant views in all directions from almost anywhere on the island. The sea is always visible and there are occasional glimpses of neighbouring islands. The sky dominates and,

thankfully, bad weather can be seen long before it arrives. A feeling of isolation, being on the fringe, was always with me. London, even Edinburgh seemed another world away.

About five hundred people live this detached life on Sanday, with the population being roughly half Orcadians and half incomers. The only part of the island you could call built up is Lady, the small village at the island's centre. Most live a field or so away from their neighbours in small farmhouses and on crofts that are fairly evenly distributed across the island.

It seems to me that the more inaccessible or remote a place in Britain is, the kinder and more welcoming the people who live there are. The first

Burness and Lamaness Firth

time I went out in my car the other drivers, of whom there were very few, waved. I drove past a house where a woman was hanging out a line of washing and she waved too.

On my second day here I telephoned a farmer to see if I could call on him to ask a few questions. I found his number in one of those 'where to go and what to see locally' folders you find in hotel rooms. In places like this I often wonder what everyday life is like so far from … well, almost everything most of us take for granted.

'Best organic farm in Britain, tours by appointment', it said. He didn't know who this total stranger was calling him out of the blue, but nevertheless arranged to see me the following morning for coffee.

I was there for more than four hours. People here are extraordinarily friendly.

The farm has 53 organic hectares, a little less than Sanday's average.

Originally outsiders, the couple have been farming here since the late 1970s, buying the farm unseen on the strength of a few photographs and never having farmed or been to Sanday, or even Orkney, before. Both were keen to get out of the Home Counties rat-race in the days of the television sitcom *The Good Life*; they wanted to become self-sufficient and began with just a few hectares of oats and a cow with a calf.

With help and advice from local farmers and by learning from their mistakes they built up the farm and eventually made it work. They now have 40 cattle and have kept chickens, sheep, ducks, pigs and a goat. They grow their own vegetables using half the remaining area and keep pigs on the other half, changing them round the following year.

To supplement their income they have fished commercially, lobsters mostly, with up to 40 pots (the full-time fishermen will have about 1,000), mowed the island's three churchyards four times a year and done odd bits of building work to be paid for in bales of hay. Dinner that day was to be a couple of ducks shot the previous evening on a walk along the beach while looking for driftwood with which they heat their house.

Before you begin to feel envious, take into account the fact that winter was upon them (out here it lasts from November to May), which meant that the animals must be kept indoors and every day, whatever the weather, they would be occupied with mucking out. This takes three hours and also they must feed them twice.

From all this enterprise they have not made enough money to be called an income, no-one does, but they have achieved their goal; they have survived and enjoyed it.

Although Sanday is tree-less it is surrounded by forests, but you are only likely to see these at the very lowest tides, or as I did, after a good storm. These are forests of laminaria, better known as the seaweed kelp.

Whitemill Bay is a mile-long, north facing beach of white shell fragments at the end of Sanday's northerly peninsula, Burness. The locals call the beach Riv after The Riv, the rocks that project northward into the sea off its western end. I found about twenty per cent of the beach covered in the brown fronds and thick stalks of kelp that had been torn from the sea-bed by the storm and cast ashore in piles that are known here as tangles.

Many generations of Sanday residents have collected these tangles, stacking them to dry on stone platforms they call steethes, which can been found at many places round the island on the headlands or, as here, nestling amongst the dunes behind the beach. When the tangles have dried they are shipped to Lochmaddy on North Uist in the Western Isles, where they are processed to extract alginates used in the food processing, textile, cosmetic and pharmaceutical industries.

Life out here is elemental, I would say. For my Sanday landlady that word would describe the island well, but with a different meaning.

She believes physical illness to be the last resort of our spirit calling attention to matters in our lives that need to be resolved and that nature's energies can be utilised to help us heal ourselves. Around Sanday she has identified locations that have particular natural properties and runs a retreat for those who come here to be helped in that way or just to relax away from the hurly-burly of modern life. One of these locations is Riv, which she described to me as "a powerful beach".

She says that as the beach faces north it is the place physically to work out negative feelings such as anger, jealousy and hatred. It is also a good beach for saying final goodbyes, by writing in the sand messages of intent that will eventually be washed away by the sea.

I must admit that I felt relaxed here, in tune with nature even, but I find that happens on almost any beach, especially when they are as quiet, isolated and beautiful as this. If I had been inclined to write a message in the sand at Riv it would not have been a final goodbye, more 'au revoir Sanday'.

NORTH BY EAST

BERWICK-UPON-TWEED
NORTHUMBERLAND

It would be fair to describe Berwick as historic. If other towns can make that claim merely because they have a charter dating back to the year dot, or because a Roman road is thought to lie somewhere underground, or maybe because some ancient remains were discovered when a multi-storey car park was being built, then Berwick deserves that title more than most.

Berwick even looks historic. Built across a natural headland on the north side of the River Tweed where it enters the North Sea, the town is encircled by substantial defensive walls which suggest a less tranquil past than it enjoys today.

The town has an unspoilt appearance, having been spared the less attractive alterations and developments that many towns have suffered in the last fifty years or so.

If it were much further south it would no doubt be a popular destination for those wishing to get away from the usual English townscape, to experience somewhere that is more gentle on the eyes. Having said that, it could not be described as pretty. Rye or Stow-on-the-Wold it is not, but it is attractive, even picturesque in places; if in a slightly dour Scottish kind of way. Think of it as a small, grey Bath or Harrogate.

Its Scottishness is what makes it unique, as an English town.

It seems somehow fitting that the railway line running through Berwick will take you north to Waverley station in Edinburgh or south to Kings Cross in London. Alight onto one of Berwick's platforms and you will be standing on the site of the former Great Hall of Berwick Castle, where in 1292 King Edward I arbitrated in a dispute between Robert Bruce VI (grandfather of Robert *the* Bruce), John de Baliol and several others over their various claims to the Scottish Crown. He settled in favour of the Englishman Baliol, seeing how you ask.

Berwick's position put it in the front line during a succession of border wars between England and Scotland through the Middle Ages and the town changed hands 13 times. It was part of the ransom paid by William the Lion of Scotland to Henry II in 1147, was sold to the Scots by Richard I to help fund the Crusades and was destroyed by King John in 1216.

Although some remains of the town's earliest defences begun by Edward II can still be seen, the walls are mostly from the early years of the reign of Elizabeth I when the alliance between Scotland and France brought fears of an invasion. At the time the

walls were the latest thing in defence technology, designed for the effective delivery and survival of gunpowder artillery. They are the only example of this type, an Italian design, in Britain and one of the earliest in Europe and as such are of interest from a European military history point of view. Their survival is possibly due in some part to the fact that they were never put to the test.

Berwick was last a Scottish town in 1482 when it was taken by the Duke of Gloucester, who became Richard III the following year. Eventually, by a treaty between Mary Queen of Scots and Edward VI, it became a semi-autonomous city state-like independent borough 'The County of the Borough and Town of Berwick-upon-Tweed', having to be specifically mentioned as a separate entity in any Act of Parliament relating to affairs between England and Scotland.

Now it is in the English county of Northumberland, while over the border in Scotland is the former county of Berwickshire, joined with Selkirk and Roxboroughshire to make Scottish Borders Council.

Berwick appears to ignore the sea. Instead it faces south, making a striking sight as it huddles defiantly on the headland behind its powerful fortifications, overlooking England and Scotland's natural border the River Tweed, that glides grandly round it, broad and moat-like.

The entry into the town from the south is dramatic however you arrive. Three bridges sweep across the Tweed together, each one a superb example of the ever-changing art of the engineer and looking stunning as a group.

The oldest, 15 low, pink sandstone arches of varying width and the nearest to the sea was, appropriately, built by the king who united the thrones of England and Scotland, James I or VI depending on where you are reading this. Upstream is Robert Stephenson's Royal Border Bridge, a one and a quarter mile long viaduct carrying the railway 37 metres above the Tweed on 28 tall and elegant arches, opened by Queen Victoria in 1850. Between them in height and position the A1 crosses the river on the four long arches of the Royal Tweed Bridge, built of concrete in 1928.

Arriving across the latter I somehow found my way through a maze of narrow streets to a car park on an old quayside by the Tweed, just downstream from the Jacobean bridge.

From there I retraced my route back into the town centre in search of a telephone box to report home. When working alone I am conscious of the fact that for most of the time no-one knows where I am. If something should happen, for instance a cliff I am working on could collapse into the sea – it does happen – who would know that I could be there buried under several tons of material?

After making my call I stepped out of the telephone box and heard someone shout from across the road, "Peter Collyer, what are you doing here?"

Having just listened to one familiar voice from the other end of the country in Wiltshire, I was somewhat taken aback to then hear another I associated with the same distant town.

This was someone who until recently had worked at my local town hall, whom I got to know on my occasional visits there to peruse the latest batch of planning applications on behalf of our civic society. I knew that she was from this part of the country and had recently moved back here, but found it difficult to comprehend the fact that I had just travelled more than 400 miles to be here and we

55°46.0'N 1°59.3'W

Lowry Shelter

remark, "Well at least in Berwick you can buy a pair of knickers".

All the changes of border made me wonder what people here considered themselves to be. What do I call someone from Berwick? A Berwicker, apparently. And do Berwickers consider themselves to be English or Scottish, or is it neither or both?

In most cases probably just a Berwicker, but it really depends on your ancestry. You will hear some people from here with English accents and some with Scottish, and they are generally very tolerant of others.

I also wondered why Berwick was so often the pawn in border disputes and why it became so important. My friends informed me that at one time Berwick was Scotland's wealthiest burgh and leading port, so was worth fighting over. Trade with Europe was big. At one time a lot of merchants from the Low Countries lived here and wool was exported from here to there. Dutch or Flemish was once a common language and children went from here to a Scottish University over there.

I had noticed that the town faces the river and that not much is made of the land overlooking the sea. A harbour on the river would have been more sheltered, both for the ships and the buildings of the original town, out of the wind off the North Sea. The harbour was still busy with the fishing fleet until the sixties, when the herrings went from the North Sea. There's still some shipping in and out, some of it from Russia. Things like fertiliser and cement are brought in and grain and stone taken out.

The area I would be painting was on the quiet side of town, down by the harbour pier.

"Yes," said my friend. "Rebuilt in the early eighteen hundreds. You might see someone walking a dog, that's all."

both just happened to be in the same part of Hide Hill in Berwick-upon-Tweed at the same time.

Explanations over, I was then taken on a guided tour of the town which included a visit to a rather modest looking shelter close to a beach behind the pier, the subject of a 1959 L.S. Lowry painting *On the Sands*. Many may know Lowry only for his work in and around his native Salford, but apparently he holidayed and painted in Berwick for many years and it was not until the local council planned to demolish the derelict building that his link with the town came to light. Saved by the efforts of Berwick Civic Society and Berwick Preservation Trust, the shelter has now been preserved as part of a newly created Berwick-upon-Tweed Lowry Trail.

Eventually we met with my friend's husband who grew up in Berwick. We chatted for a while about Wiltshire and their move. Berwick is a similar size town to my own, but has few other towns of any great size within about 60 miles, whereas in Wiltshire we are surrounded by similar towns and also have Bath, Bristol and Swindon only a short car ride away. I wondered how the two places compared. My analysis was summed up by her

NORTH-NORTH-EAST

BOULMER

NORTHUMBERLAND

It has the appearance of being a small fishing hamlet. The locals pronounce it *boomer*.

A road runs north/south roughly parallel with the beach. For about a quarter of a mile along its landward side there is a small collection of modern and Edwardian bungalows. At the northern end overlooking the beach are some small older houses, a pub, the *Fishing Boat Inn*, and a barn with the parish notice board attached. There is a church called St Andrews that holds services on the first Sunday of each month, a non-RNLI lifeboat station (although the RNLI was here from 1825 to 1968), a coastguard equipment store, a BT telephone box, an EIIR post box on a pole, a public convenience (what a relief!) and four bus stops, one with a substantial stone shelter.

It's very quiet here. Depending on when you come you might see the postman doing his rounds in his red van, or even catch the wheelie bins being emptied. You might even witness the relative pandemonium of some cattle being herded down the road into a nearby farmyard for milking. If you listen carefully you might occasionally hear the call of oystercatchers.

You would never know, therefore, just by looking and listening. The only clue is in the initials of the pub's name, but in the beach here at Boulmer is New York. Yes, New York, so good they named it twice, as the song goes.

By New York I do not mean *the* New York. Frank Sinatra didn't sing about this one. Why should he? He probably never even knew it existed. This is *a* New York. A metropolis teaming with well-fed bodies and life that is bigger and better than anywhere else around. People come from as far away as Sunderland (55 miles) and even Hartlepool (75 miles) to be a part of it.

The sands at Boulmer, of course, are not quite substantial enough to hold a human population the size of New York's. This is your Big Apple only if you are … a lugworm. If you are one, beware. Those visitors from the towns and cities down the coast with their adult-size buckets and spades are not here to amuse themselves building skyscrapers of sand. They are here to dig you up for bait, so make sure you do not end up top of their heap.

Boulmer Haven is a natural safe mooring enclosed by a broken circle of offshore rocks. It had a reputation for being a great gin smuggling centre and some of the older houses are thought to have secret cellars for hiding the booty. The main offshore

55°25.1'N 1°34.7'W

activity today seems to be fishing. Moored in the Haven and parked up on trailers at the head of the beach are a number of cobles, small traditional fishing boats peculiar to the North Sea coast of northern England. These days it is good to see working fishing boats of any kind, so when, with the odd exception, they are of the local vernacular it's especially heartwarming.

Occasionally you may catch sight of an appropriately named Sea King search and rescue helicopter (seeking; get it?). You can't really miss them. They are big and yellow with a fuselage shaped like a boat's hull. You are more likely to hear the roar of the engines and deep thud of the rotor blades before one comes into sight. A brace are stationed at RAF Boulmer just inland from the hamlet.

As RAF bases go Boulmer is quite small. The Sea Kings fly from a small part of the site which is the original World War II grass airfield, with the other two thirds of their squadron operated by colleagues based at RAF Lossiemouth and Normandy Army Barracks at Leconfield, near Beverley. Between them they will fly about 600 sorties a year, saving the lives of more than 500 people.

From Boulmer they could be winching the crew off a sinking fishing boat 100 miles out in the North Sea one day and searching for missing climbers in the Lake District or the Borders the next.

Most RAF personnel based here, however, are assigned to the Air Surveillance and Control System, which monitors all aircraft flying in and around UK military air space, or to the School of Fighter Control which trains them for that task. They rehearse directing RAF fighters to intercept incoming enemy aircraft, wherever they may come from.

During the cold war that threat was presumed to be the Soviet Union, that is why there are so many more stations like Boulmer on the East coast. In those days the real thing would come along occasionally and play a game of cat and mouse with them. An obsolete grey Phantom jet stands inside one of the gates into the base as a monument to those times.

Just beyond the barrier at the main gate was – from a civilian's point of view – an enigmatic sign. It conveyed two pieces of information. One was the NBC Dress Category and the other the Bikini State. I puzzled over these for a while. If they were related, maybe it referred to a civilian clothes concession day. Somehow I could not imagine airmen wearing bikinis in October, at least not in Northumberland.

Eventually my curiosity got the better of me. Watched over by an airman carrying an automatic weapon I went to the small window at the guard room and popped my question, having first handed over my driving licence for them to take down some details. Apparently NBC refers to the different types of protective clothing they would wear in the case of an emergency, or exercise: Nuclear, Biological or Chemical.

"And what about Bikini State?" I asked. "You're not pretending this is Hawaii."

"That's a secret."

"Is it an acronym?" I pressed, thinking we could play along with this for a while. There didn't seem to be much else to do.

"I can't say."

I tried a different approach. "Do you have a press officer I could speak to?"

"You could write to the Officer Commanding," was the reply. I took this as a polite 'Please go away' and went down to the beach to watch the lugworm diggers at work.

Boulmer - Sunset

The population of this outpost outnumber the civilian residents many times. Whereas down by the sea you could imagine that everyone is from a local family going back many generations, those stationed at RAF Boulmer are essentially transitory. Two or three years and then you are moved on to another posting, hardly having had time to get to know the place. That might explain why some rarely leave the base at all to mix with the local community. You could be ill, entertained, fed and watered, married and have children without ever passing beyond the perimeter fence: never knowing that you could buy a crab from a local fisherman, have a good pint or two in the FBI, or dig for the biggest, juiciest lugworms you're ever likely to drown on the end of a line.

The afternoon of my arrival at Boulmer coincided with a period of calm sandwiched between several days of heavy squally showers. The approach of dusk, with the setting sun reflecting off clouds to the east was absolutely stunning. I knew at the time that I was experiencing something special and this tranquil time was my abiding memory of the visit.

On the day I started the painting back in my studio there was a programme on television about the long period of heavy rain and flooding that many parts of the country were experiencing. During the programme a live report from the Met. Office announced "The wettest place in Britain today was Boulmer". I could close my eyes and just imagine it. Bikini State? Sou'wester State more like.

NORTH-EAST BY NORTH

TYNEMOUTH
TYNE AND WEAR

My one previous visit to Tynemouth was on a grey May bank holiday. Gale force winds brought in waves that leapt over the promenade railings with the ease and frequency of athletes competing in the heats of the 110 metres hurdles at the Olympics. On that occasion every layer of clothing received a good soaking. It was not a jolly experience.

The painting I made recording the conditions on that occasion was bought by someone who grew up nearby and said that it always seemed to be like that. Somehow I had managed to paint his memory of the place.

This current visit brought back my memory of it. It was autumn and again we had strong winds. On this occasion the waves just failed to clear the hurdles. However, I managed to be caught out by a particularly heavy shower. There was nowhere to shelter and the rain fell like it had been fired from a water cannon.

I had driven here from Boulmer, keeping to roads that took me as near as possible to the coast. It was not a pleasant journey. In bad weather almost anywhere can look a trifle grim and quite by chance I had chosen what seemed to be the least attractive route possible to my destination. Once there, I sat for a while in my rapidly misting up car waiting for the rain to stop, eventually giving up and driving into North Shields in search of the tourist information office.

There I bought a postcard reproduction of a 1931 Alfred Lambart poster for the London and North Eastern Railway. A young man in a russet coloured blazer and white slacks sits on a cliff top, his arms clasped round his legs hugging his knees against his chest. On a bench behind him sits a young woman in a yellow blouse and black skirt, shielding herself from the blazing sun with a Japanese style parasol casually held over her left shoulder. Behind her, in a white sleeveless dress and white cloche hat stands another young woman. They gaze down dreamily onto the golden beach below where people are sun-bathing and swimming. In the distance, overlooking the beach and set against a clear deep blue sky stands a grand building. It looks like a scene on the Côte d'Azur. In large letters across the top of the poster is written the word TYNEMOUTH.

In my experience this is what is known as artistic licence.

Perhaps I should have come in July.

Tynemouth stands on a headland on the north side of, as its name indicates, the mouth of the River Tyne. It merges seamlessly into Cullercoats and Whitley Bay to the north and North Shields to the west. These towns and villages are just a small part of a massive conurbation which most outsiders would simply refer to as Newcastle or Tyneside, including such places as Jarrow, Gateshead, South Shields, Wallsend and Gosforth; all names that those with a long memory will associate with heavy industry and shipbuilding.

Of all the places that make up the Tyne and Wear region, Tynemouth is the one to visit for the best views and people have been coming here to enjoy them for more than two hundred years. A panorama of the coastline on either side of the Tyne can be viewed by taking a walk along the North Tyne pier that protects the mouth of the river by extending more than half a mile out into the North Sea. The pier is a very substantial piece of masonry, but on windy days waves will clear this comfortably, too.

I came out here for some exercise and to take in the views when it eventually stopped raining, or so I had thought. Do not even think about putting up a brolly or it will definitely be the last time you use it. This is where the water cannon struck.

Looking around the town you could be forgiven for thinking that nothing of any great consequence existed in Tynemouth before the beginning of the nineteenth century, a century which saw rapid development over the whole Tyneside area. Buildings from that period dominate the townscape and are a reminder of the wealth that Tyne industries and trade generated in those days. However, there is one view which takes us much further back, through many centuries to times when power was in different hands.

Front Street is a wide thoroughfare leading from Tynemouth's centre, joining the coast road from Cullercoats at the point where a headland projects from the cliffs, near the landward end of the pier. The eastern prospect of Front Street is dominated by the dramatic view of the fourteenth century barbican and gatehouse of Tynemouth Castle. The whole headland is heavily fortified with substantial curtain walls, especially across the neck of land between the headland and the town. Pass through the gatehouse, however, and you will find that inside the walls of the castle stand the ruins of Tynemouth Priory.

For much of the time I spent here I had the place to myself, which was not really surprising as the weather was so unpleasant. Once inside I noticed that the sky was beginning to brighten, there may even, eventually, be some sunshine...

A great deal of my visit was spent wandering around the ruins with the very informative English Heritage guide book, looking for a paintable view, especially one which might benefit from a few rays of sunshine, and trying to imagine what the site was like when the priory and castle were flourishing.

I found the latter somewhat difficult. I am afraid it is my usual response to remains as scant as these. I can be roused to pathos, saddened by the loss of a community and its splendid architecture (although it is usually the stained glass windows that I enjoy the most in ecclesiastical buildings), but I find putting together in my mind a three dimensional building from a few sections of ruined wall like trying to imagine a living dinosaur when given a fossilised tooth to look at.

55°01.1'N 1°24.9'W

Priory's headland from the pier

symbols of the powers they once represented and even in ruins they make uneasy companions.

Eventually I found a view I liked and after a long wait the sun even came out.

I stood against what was left of the north wall of the nave looking east. In the foreground the remains of the priory church's west front cast a shadow across the bases of three columns. In sunlight stood the solid wall of the rood screen and behind it the three surviving piers that once supported the tower at the crossing of the nave and the transepts, together with one arch of the south transept. This part of the building was constructed between 1090 and 1140. Behind all this rises the most impressive section of the ruins, the 22 metre high east end of the early thirteenth century presbytery. It seems likely that this survived because of its usefulness as a waymark for shipping. In the distance, across the mouth of the river is the South Tyne pier and beyond that the North Sea.

By the time I left I was feeling some sympathy for the Benedictine monks who once occupied this headland. As I discovered from the guide book while waiting for the sun to come out, apart from the kitchen, the small warming house between the refectory and chapter house was the only room on the whole site where a fire was allowed. It was very cold indeed.

I should definitely have been here in July.

Much of the site is now open and grassed over, but one thing that is quite clear from the guide book is that until very recently the headland was crammed with a great number of buildings; accommodation and agricultural buildings for the priory, domestic and administrative for the castle. In fact, military occupation of the site continued until after the Second World War and the barracks, huts, store rooms and magazines were not removed until 1960.

The grouping of the remains, with the castle's at the western end of the site and the priory's on the open grassed area in the centre, with views beyond along the coast and out to sea, creates both a picturesque scene and a somewhat haunting atmosphere. Both sets of remains are striking

NORTH-EAST

HORDEN
COUNTY DURHAM

NASA's Mars Pathfinder mission took seven months to reach our outer neighbour, arriving (didn't it just have to?) on 4 July 1997. When its incredible photographs of the Martian landscape were shown for the first time on television I watched in wonder. At the time I, too, was in an unfamiliar neighbouring land, in Denmark, after a modestly epic seven day journey, travelling from Newcastle upon Tyne via Norway, the Faeroe Islands and Iceland for my first book *Rain Later, Good*, an account of my travels round the Shipping Forecast.

I had a similar 'gazing-in-wonder at something outer-planetary-like' experience when I first took that one small step onto the beach at Horden. This time I was only 23 miles from Newcastle but I could have been 49 million.

The previous night had been spent with an old school friend now living in Durham. When I told him why I was in the area he said with an expression that fell somewhere between cynicism and incredulity:

"I can't imagine what you are going to find to paint in Horden."

Through most of the twentieth century County Durham's prosperity was founded on the mining of coal. Now the eight collieries along the county's 12 mile stretch of coast have all closed and there is a tangible air of depression in the area.

Leaving the main road through Horden village where my instinct told me, I stumbled by chance upon the road that took me down to the sea. After passing under the bridge carrying the Sunderland to Hartlepool railway line the scenery changes suddenly from turn of the twentieth century red brick urban to rural. Descending a single-track lane through a narrow wooded valley I passed a National Trust sign indicating that this was Dene Mouth and soon arrived at a small car park by a fast flowing stream next to the beach. So here I was on planet Horden.

Taking in the scene for those first few minutes I understood why my friend had made his remark.

The wide beach is quite unlike any I had seen before. Near the cliffs is an almost flat area strewn with large sea-rounded rocks, light in colour and coated to varying degrees in a rust coloured deposit. Halfway down the beach is a ridge, below which it slopes towards the sea becoming a dark brown/grey mixture of sand and shale scattered with a few green/grey pebbles. There was something not quite natural about the environment I found myself in.

This is not entirely surprising when you consider that the collieries used the beach for dumping their spoil.

Before mechanisation in the mid-twentieth century, when production was measured in hundreds of tonnes per week, the sea managed to remove the spoil quite well. There was not too much of it as miners were only paid for the coal they sent to the surface, not for the waste. After mechanisation brought production up to thousands of tonnes per week the spoil began to accumulate as each tonne of coal produced two tonnes of waste. The machines are less discriminating than the men.

In all, the accumulated spoil along the length of the Durham coast has been estimated to amount to about two hundred million tonnes.

Iron oxide and sulphurous material in the slurry from the coal washing process was pumped onto the beach causing the discolouration I had noticed on the existing natural beach material.

Since the colliery closures, the National Trust has acquired almost half of the Durham coast. The purchase of Horden beach was something of a watershed for the Neptune Campaign. It is certainly not the sort of property that would have been on their original shopping list. Not that it broke the bank as British Coal let them have it for £1.

Together with more than a dozen other organisations, including councils, conservation groups and statutory bodies in a £10 million regeneration project known as *Turning The Tide*, the Trust has begun the long process of enabling mother nature to restore the coast to something resembling its pre-industrial appearance.

The once coal-blackened beaches are now beginning to take on a more natural sandy hue as the sea slowly removes the lightweight shale, replacing it with the heavier sand. In time the sea will eat into the spoil; moving back to the base of the cliffs the ridge that separates the two sections of beach.

I began to walk northward along the shore in search of a subject for my painting. On my right a slight swell brought silty waves ashore with an occasional crash. On my left was the beach from underground, backed by a line of grass-covered cliffs.

Apparently nearly 100,000 people live within a mile or so of the Durham coast. On such a lovely bright October morning after several days of wind and rain it was disappointing to find that I was almost alone, sharing the calm only with two young men setting up their rods for a spot of sea angling.

The cliffs here form an almost uniformly straight ridge. The colliery spoil has raised the level of the beach so much that the sea no longer reaches the base of the cliffs, so halting the process of erosion and allowing grass to grow over them, thus creating a sloping green wall. At first I passed cliffs which were of boulder clay, a glacial deposit from the last ice age. In places the cliff face has slumped and then grassed over again creating a rolling, undulating effect.

As I progressed north I approached a natural break in the cliff line and beyond this the clay could be seen to be sitting on a two to three metre high wall of limestone, not just any old limestone, but magnesian limestone, no less. The grassland associated with it is a rare habitat indeed. In fact 75 per cent of the mere 274 hectares of it in the whole of Britain are in the east of County Durham, with 50 per cent of it here on this stretch of coast. *Turning The Tide* has been recreating this habitat along the coast, in some cases replacing arable land with it, so when the erosion of the cliffs eventually begins again the

54°46.1'N 1°18.0'W

wildlife communities will have a natural grassland zone in which to retreat.

This break in the cliffs was Blackhills Gill, a small valley cut through the boulder clay by a stream, that spreads out a river delta-like fan of channels as it crosses the sandy part of the beach into the sea.

At this point I walked up the beach to the ridge and discovered that the rocks there have created a dam, holding back some of the stream's flow forming a pool or lakelet. With the view through the mouth of the Gill as a backdrop the scene was almost pretty, in an austere sort of way. At last I had found my subject.

On my way back to the car I met a little dog leading a man in his mid fifties who walked with the aid of a stick. I noticed that there were two small enamel badges pinned to the man's woolly hat; one bore the deep blue star of Newcastle Breweries and the other the oak leaf and acorn of the National Trust: an interesting pairing of symbols. We had a brief

conversation about the state of the beach and each other's accents, mine indicating that I was obviously not a local and his that he was. I told him that I was a Collyer but it had nothing to do with mining coal, then he told me something about life working underground at Horden colliery.

He had worked underground for 26 years until the colliery closed in 1987. The coal-face was nearly a mile down and extended up to five miles out under the sea. At least they were paid for their underground travelling time.

Conditions were cold and wet underground. Oilskins and wellies were worn and much of the work was done on hands and knees. He now has arthritis in his knees; hence the walking stick. Cold water from a natural underground reservoir would drip off the roof and down the miners' backs. The water had a salinity seven times that of sea water, so not only did their bodies become blackened with coal dust but also streaked white with salt deposits. Despite all this he felt that conditions were not that bad. What he misses most is "the crack".

Coal cutting by then was done by machine, each day being different enough to exercise the mind and prevent the job from becoming boring or tedious, unlike today's repetitive factory work that is now the sort of job on offer locally; not that he felt he has much chance there. With still a decade to go to retirement he considers himself unemployable. Even the young have difficulty finding work here.

The beach restoration work at Horden is wonderful and uplifting, giving the people here something to enjoy which the past few generations have missed out on and they can be proud of what has been created. Given the choice, however, I am sure they would rather have their livelihoods back.

Coal beach at Horden

NORTH-EAST BY EAST

COATHAM, REDCAR
REDCAR & CLEVELAND

I want a big "aah" for the folks of Coatham, poor dears they just don't know where they are. Until 1899 they were little old Coatham on their own and then they suddenly found themselves joined with neighbouring Redcar, with which there had been much rivalry.

In those days they were, and had been for centuries, part of the largest county in England. Yorkshire had been divided by the Danes (appropriate here as this becomes a bit of a saga) into North, East and West Ridings, a riding being derived from the Danish word *treding* meaning a third part, with Coatham and Redcar firmly in the North Riding.

In 1968 the shiny new county of Teeside was created by slicing Redcar (and Coatham of course) off the Yorkshire map along with Middlesbrough, joining them with places like Stockton-on-Tees, which had thought it was in County Durham. As a lower tier of government within Teeside they became Redcar and Coatham Urban District Council.

A mere blink of a civil servant's eye later, as part of the 1974 general reorganisation of local government (which saw the loss of Rutland and the creation of Avon, for instance) Redcar (not forgetting Coatham) became part of the new county of Cleveland, taking its name from the highest range of hills in the North York Moors National Park. Redcar and Coatham UDC then disappeared to be replaced with Langbaurgh (pronounced *langbarth*) Borough Council, named like Milton Keynes after the smallest community in the area. Later the name had to be changed to Langbaugh-on-Tees so people knew where it was.

Are you still with me?

In 1996 Cleveland ceased to exist as a county, being replaced by four unitary authorities one of them being Redcar and Cleveland Borough Council. At least Redcar regained its name, but we seem to have lost Coatham altogether.

A significant result of the last change is that although they now have a council that does everything a county does, they are now county-less. Write to someone in Coatham and you do not have a county to address the envelope with, just a boring TS (Teeside) postcode.

As I found when I quizzed the nice lady at Redcar and Cleveland's Kirkleatham Museum:

"Feelings on this matter run very high. Older folks who can still remember the good old days of the

54°37.2'N 1°05.2'W

North Riding of Yorkshire will still refer to 'North Yorks' with a tear in the eye."

Strangely enough there is now a North Yorkshire County Council, but I won't go into that.

"Younger people not so wedded to the concept of Yorkshire are reluctant to let go of Cleveland and continue to claim they live there."

All I can say is, remember to use the postcode.

I arrived at Redcar on the seventeenth day of my tour round the compass points and it was the first day without rain. In fact, the sun shone out of a clear blue sky from dawn to dusk and the temperature was unseasonally hot. If it had not been for the typical seaside town Englishness of the place it would have been positively Mediterranean.

Coatham/Redcar is not the prettiest coastal resort I have visited, neither is it the ugliest, but on the whole like many others it is fairly unremarkable and therefore could be quite forgettable, but it is smart in a modest sort of way. I wandered up and down the esplanade a couple of times to take in the atmosphere and one thing soon became obvious, Redcar makes great play of the 'red' element of its name. They really have painted the town ... what else but red, of course; red lamp-posts, red flag poles, red esplanade railings.

The latter are home to an interesting gallery of images depicting scenes from local life, industry and history and a few illustrating nursery rhymes, no doubt for the younger viewers. What makes these unusual is that each element within a picture; the figures, machines, the sea etc were all cut from sheet metal, welded together and then painted, telling their individual story in a light-hearted cartoon style. There is something of the seaside postcard about them, this is public art at its most enjoyable and accessible.

Having been involved with public art projects in my home town I was intrigued to discover more about the panels and tracked down a planning officer who was involved in the project. They were created during the regime of the previous authority Langbaugh, but although the name has changed, fortunately the people haven't.

Probably the most telling remark came in his opening sentence,

"Redcar was a resort town."

It may still be a place for a race meeting or a day trip from the nearby metropolis of Middlesbrough, but few regard it now as a holiday destination. Aware of the need to do something about the town's steady decline, an examination of the borough was commissioned to look at what it was doing, how it was performing and what was needed to make improvements that would draw people back.

As is often the case, little of the cash from Westminster and Brussels the consultants suggested applying for materialised, nevertheless some of the schemes that were proposed went ahead with local funding. Public art was seen as a vehicle for urban design change so these wonderful panels, "a reflection of Redcar" as the council officer aptly described them, went ahead as part of a scheme of improvements to the esplanade.

Whether they are thought of as high art, just a bit of fun, or a waste of tax-payers money, they are seen, enjoyed and, importantly, remembered as being what makes Redcar different and special. They reflect well on the town, so they do their job, alone worth making the trip for. Well done all concerned, particularly their creator Chris Topp.

Along the esplanade there was everything I expected to find in a small resort, plus one or two

things I didn't, including in the old lifeboat station a small museum dedicated to the *Zetland*, the oldest purpose-built lifeboat in the world, built in 1802 and in service until 1880. The town has something else to be proud of and to shout about (which they are and do).

Opposite the new RNLI station a couple of cobles were parked on trailers, a reminder that Coatham and Redcar were once neighbouring fishing villages, with Coatham being the more important port in mediaeval times. It is difficult to imagine all that now, though.

At the end of the nineteenth century this short walk along the sea front would have taken me from Redcar's to Coatham's piers. These came to represent the rivalry between the two towns and were both long in length but short in life. Coatham's lasted 25 years, being wrecked in a storm before it was finished and finally almost completely destroyed when another storm drove a barque through it. Three years before that event fire broke out in Redcar's pier and the first fire brigade to arrive on the scene was Coatham's, but mysteriously they could not manage to pump any water from the sea. Oh, dear! It's burnt down. Merger of the two towns was opposed by a 'hands off Redcar' campaign. I'm not surprised.

It was impossible to tell where I had passed from one town into the other, but soon I came to the end of the sea wall and found myself in the natural landscape of Coatham Dunes, with a broad sandy beach in front of me and on this rare occasion a blue North Sea beyond. If it wasn't for the caravan park behind me, the nearby steel-works and the tankers passing in and out of the Teeside oil refineries and chemical plants I could almost have been on a tropical desert island.

Sun, sand and ... steel

EAST-NORTH-EAST

WHITBY

NORTH YORKSHIRE

I will come to Whitby in a moment, but first I need to make a confession.

I am not that interested in art.

Well, maybe I am, but not as much as I think I should be, it's a passive interest rather than an active one. I am not one for going round galleries, but do it occasionally. I think the problem is that I find it difficult to see beyond the technical aspects of its creation. On the whole I am probably just not that interested in what other artists are up to, but this may be because subconsciously I think of them as competition and would rather not see how good they are. Discuss.

Over the last few years, however, I have become more aware of how many great British watercolour painters there were in the nineteenth century and, I'm glad to say, I enjoy looking at their work and discovering another I had not previously been aware of. For this I can thank Chris Beetles.

Chris sells my work at the gallery in St James's, London, that bears his name and I am proud to be associated with him. It's not your average gallery and he's not your average gallery owner.

Chris Beetles Ltd is a cornucopia of works on paper where you will find Albert Goodwin and W.

Heath Robinson hanging around together. I find that time spent browsing there is as rewarding as at any public or private collection.

He knows his art, but arrived where he is today by an unusual route. Chris has been a General Practioner and half of the comedy double act Beetles and Buckman (coincidentally, Rob Buckman was at medical college with my own doctor) who had a television series *The Pink Medicine Show* which you might remember. However, he has long had a passion for paintings and is now recognised as a leading authority on watercolours, although he "came into watercolours like Atilla the Hun", as he likes to put it.

Being told by Chris in such inspiring surroundings that my work has something Pre-Raphaelite about it is a humbling experience.

It was here that I discovered the work of a painter who I consider to be the best nineteenth century British watercolourist, Alfred William Hunt.

He made his first painting expedition to Whitby in 1874 and is thought to have returned there every year until his death in 1896. There were particular areas of the town that he liked to revisit, one of them being the roof of the railway station and another

Spion Kop, the hillside above Pier Road on the west side of the harbour.

I was unaware of this at the time, so it is pure coincidence that I also chose the latter as the place from which to do my painting one gloriously warm and sunny May evening. Well it is a great (and hardly changed) view looking across the harbour to some of the oldest buildings in the town, including the remains of the Abbey, even if the plaque on the bench here says 'The view from this spot inspired Bram Stoker (1847–1912)'.

I can understand why Hunt returned so often. Whitby is fascinating. A small country would be content with the town's history. The smell of its maritime past hangs heavy in the air and is as pervasive as that of fresh, smoked and cooked fish. It can do the touristy thing better than most towns, catering for all kinds of holiday needs: beach, cliffs, great views, historic buildings, interesting walks through quaint cobbled streets, a good collection of specialist shops, fascinating museums, a marina, steam trains even, but the lingering impression is that Whitby is still about fishing and going to sea.

The town's most famous association is with Captain James Cook, who is revered and celebrated just about everywhere between Middlesbrough and Whitby and rightly so. Cook's sea-going career began at Whitby and the ships he used for his three epic voyages of discovery in the latter half of the eighteenth century; *Endeavour* and *Resolution* accompanied by *Adventure* and *Discovery* were all built in Whitby shipyards.

The harbour is the hub of the town. Surrounded and isolated by the hills of the North York Moors National Park, the two halves of Whitby face each other as they cling to the steep slopes of the gorge that conveys the River Esk into the sea between the two high cliffs that provide the harbour with its natural shelter.

Until the construction upstream of the modern high level road bridge that keeps passing traffic out of the town centre's steep and winding streets, the site of the present Edwardian swing bridge had been the only crossing point from one side of town to the other. Though constantly busy with traffic both vehicular and pedestrian, the swing bridge is a good location at which to linger and take in the superb views of the town and its harbour.

Just downstream on the west bank at the Pier Road quayside is the fish dock, handling the catches from Whitby's small but modern trawler fleet, where the dominant building is the large shed of the fish market. By contrast, just upstream on the east bank at the end of Grape Lane is the early seventeenth century house where the young James Cook stayed when in port (now the Captain Cook Memorial Museum) and a timber jetty where a small collection of cobles are usually moored.

I have found a number of these so far on my travels and was delighted to discover that they have a fan club The Coble & Keelboat Society.

The English square sterned coble is a sailing and rowing boat, though many are now motorised, working between the Tweed and the Humber. Used primarily to drift-net for herring, set long lines and set pots for crabs and lobsters, it was designed to be launched from and landed on a beach.

The coble is, as one sports pundit might have put it, a boat of two halves. From the bows it looks almost conventional, if unusually deep and pronounced. When viewed from the stern you can see it has two side keels that start about amidships. When launching and landing they hold the boat upright

54°29.2'N 0°36.4'W

and prevent the aft from digging in to the beach. The square stern is horseshoe shaped and rakes aft at about 45°. When landing, stern first, the deep bows help to hold it steady, like a rudder would on a more conventional boat and keep it pointing into the surf.

I managed to track down the owner of the last boatyard in Whitby to be building wooden boats.

Usually he works on things like ten metre prawn trawlers, but when I spoke to him he had just started on a coble. I asked if many are built now.

"As far as I know this is the first one for eight years."

"If it's been that long, this could be the last one ever to be built then."

harbour looking north-east

"Could be, yes."

"Are you the only person to have that knowledge now?"

"No, there are others, but I'm the only one still boat building."

"What are the others doing then?"

"Working on buildings mostly."

"Don't you have an apprentice that you're handing all this knowledge on to?"

"My helper's 74, he won't be around when I pack up."

"So it could be an historic moment when this is finished and launched?"

"The BBC and ITV have both been round to see if they can film it being built, but now that I've started they really need to be here every day because it will only take seven or eight weeks."

Possibly then, I had witnessed another chapter of Whitby's maritime history being made.

However the fish landed at Whitby are caught, you will not find anywhere in Britain that will cook them better than at the Magpie Café or smoke them better than at Fortune's.

The Magpie Café, in an eighteenth century former merchant's house, pilotage and shipping office is in Pier Road right opposite the fish market. You cannot get closer to the source than that. While you tuck in to your splendid meal (after possibly queueing outside for at least half an hour before a table becomes available) you can look out of the window and see the cranes unloading the latest catch.

Although there are up to twelve varieties of fish available each day, all cooked in a great many ways, most people seem to opt for the traditional cod or haddock cooked in melt-in-the-mouth batter. I tried asking how they do it, but needless to say they wouldn't tell me. If you've tried it you'll know how good it is, if you haven't, you can't imagine.

Across the harbour in the quiet, sloping and cobbled Henrietta Street is Fortune's smoke house.

Fortune's have been smoking herrings here since 1872. When they discovered that they would have to move and make drastic changes to their shop to meet

the latest EU health regulations if they wanted to sell their kippers across Britain, they took the brave decision to stay put, keep everything as it was and only sell direct from the premises. For this we should be forever grateful and form an orderly queue all the way back to the swing bridge. You will not find anything so succulent and perfect anywhere, I felt guilty giving them such a modest sum for such a rare treat.

You might be fortune-ate to catch them at a quiet moment, if so ask nicely and I'm sure they will open the door to the smoke house and show you the magical dark world inside. The walls are thick with tar as smoke from the most modest pile of smouldering oak or beech shavings drifts up through the herrings that will hang there between 18 and 24 hours to cure.

If you are anywhere within striking distance of Whitby find the time to pay them a visit, you will not be disappointed. If you don't like smoked fish this will convert you.

Anyone reading this in Whitby can send me a well wrapped smokey parcel care of Thomas Reed Publications or Chris Beetles, both addresses in the front of the book. Thank you.

Famous
Fortunes

EAST BY NORTH

SCALBY NESS, SCARBOROUGH
NORTH YORKSHIRE

There's nothing quite like being in the right place at the right time.

Moving along the coast from one place to another does not always lead to such an ideal situation. Time spent in one place is determined entirely by how long it takes me to mooch about, get a feel for what's there, decide what my subject or subjects will be and then find an appropriate location from which to paint.

I also need time to do some background research for the text, look round a museum maybe to find out what a place is all about, or find someone who lives locally to chat to, or discover an event in the local paper, that sort of thing.

Moving on is a matter of deciding whether my time is still being productively spent, or am I just wandering about aimlessly hoping that an idea or a subject will jump out and grab me, off-guard?

The weather can also play its part. I might have spent a day somewhere with an overcast sky, which might not be the most flattering conditions for showing off the place's particular delights, if any, so if an hour or two of evening sunshine looks possible, hanging around a little longer just in case might be worth the wait.

I was lucky with my arrival at Boulmer and the view I eventually chose for my Whitby painting I found within half a minute of stepping out of my car, even though I spent another two days over the following week wandering round the town in search of more locations.

So the time of my arrival at a location is often determined by when I have finished at the previous one. It is not always perfect timing.

On this occasion I was staying for a week or so at a pretty cottage in the spectacularly picturesque village of Runswick Bay, just north of Whitby, from where I was making my painting forays up and down the Yorkshire coast. I was in the position of being able to make a fresh start at a new location and could decide where that would be once I had seen what conditions the new day would bring.

We were experiencing something of a heat-wave, very unusual for May. You probably remember it; 10th to 13th 2001. As a hot Saturday beckoned with the prospect of spending a whole day under a clear blue sky, I decided to take myself off to Scarborough, where later I might find somewhere to shelter and continue my observations under cover if I found being in the sun too unbearable.

Passing on the way just about the most walked, painted and photographed stretch of coast in the area – Robin Hood's Bay and Ravenscar – I arrived at a hazy Scarborough mid morning and made my way down to North Bay Promenade.

Suddenly, after spending days at various points along the coast working in isolation, on a deserted beach or stretch of cliff, I was reminded that normal people come to places like this purely for the fun of it, to mess about and do as they please.

The sands were liberally scattered with families on holiday, small children with buckets and spades. One heard the squirt and slap of sun tan oil being applied and saw lots of ice cream being consumed.

Scarborough is an unusual town, but I like it. There is nothing uniform about it. The western suburbs, mostly what you see if you're just passing through, could be almost anywhere, but occasionally you come across a collection of late nineteenth and early twentieth century villas that are halfway to becoming small mansions and are better than you are likely to find almost anywhere.

The more interesting parts of the town face the sea, and here it is divided in two by a one hundred metre high headland where the remains of the castle and a Roman signal station stand. The old part of the town that faces across South Bay with its working harbour is quite different to that part looking across North Bay. It's a case of 'Welcome to Scarborough – twinned with … Scarborough'.

Scarborough can claim that it is probably the original seaside resort.

In the 1620s the discovery of springs that were claimed to have healing properties led to the town becoming a spa; perhaps they should have changed its name to Spaborough. Later that century a local doctor advocated bathing in the sea and it soon became a fashionable place to take the waters in an ocean or in a glass.

From Castle Cliff, North Bay stretches away for a mile and a half. Backed by ornamental gardens its long Promenade comes to an abrupt end by a footbridge over a small river that enters the sea at this point. On the other side of the bridge is an entirely natural world of gorse covered cliffs, Scalby Ness, the headland that marks the southern boundary of the North York Moors National Park.

At high tide this could be just another headland projecting into the sea, a gentle interplay of rock and wave or at best a thundering crash of spray. At low tide it is nothing more exiting than a vast expanse of silt and sand, with a scattering of seaweed-covered rocks moistened only by the waters of the river trying to find its receded destiny.

Quite by chance I had arrived as the tide was falling and it could not have been a more perfect situation. This natural corner of North Bay was still filled with shallow water and through the sky's reflection it was possible to see still-submerged rocks between those that had become exposed by the slowly falling sea level.

Parallel with the headland a concrete culvert provided the perfect footpath across the rocks. Sea water trapped by the culvert created deep rock pools between it and the headland and a few people who had found their way out here before me wandered around slowly, heads down intently searching in them for welks or somewhere to do a little shrimping.

I, too, walked along slowly, head down, but I was looking for an interesting arrangement of rocks, a

54°17.9'N 0°24.2'W

good reflection and the best backdrop. I had to imagine my catch under glass and window-mounted behind ivory coloured card.

Locations found, I settled down and began the serious work of the day while around me the people enjoyed their lovely hot Saturday in the sun. As they passed behind with their catch-filled buckets they smiled, said "hello" and "lovely day isn't it?" and I thought, it's a perfect day, I'm glad I came here, what a great decision that was.

rock pools

EAST TO SOUTH

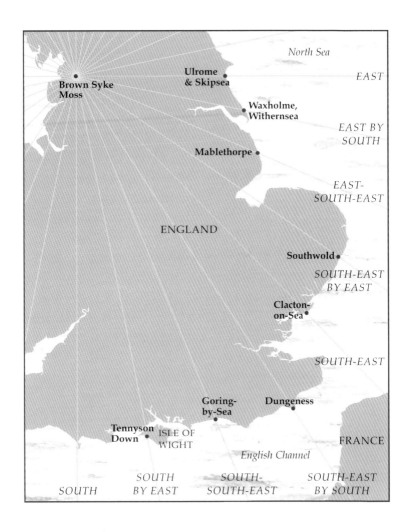

EAST

ULROME & SKIPSEA
EAST RIDING OF YORKSHIRE

Do you ever wish you could turn back the clock and live in an earlier time? I do.

Until recently, whenever I drove to London I parked my car in the street near Turnham Green Station from where I caught the tube into the centre. Alas this small pleasure is now denied me by a residents only parking scheme.

This area is the original garden suburb laid out by Richard Norman Shaw in 1878, the beginnings of 'my period', I often think to myself.

If one had lived in a newly built house there one just *had* to have the rooms decorated with the latest designs by William Morris, darling!

I am a fan of the great man. The conflict between his ideal of creating beautiful and useful hand-made things for all to enjoy and the reality of the their exclusivity because of the wealth required to afford them was something that worried him. In my own small way I can identify with that problem. Publishing my paintings in book form goes a small way to easing my conscience.

Turnham Green's great charm today is, in London terms, its sense of tranquillity and space and its glorious arboreal setting. If it wasn't for the cars (pause while I check all the definitions of *irony* in the

dictionary) you could imagine you were still in Morris's time.

I am fascinated too by the 1950s, possibly because I lived through some of the decade. I catch up with it by watching films of the period and often find myself thinking 'if only things were like that now, they seemed so innocent and honest'. There's a scene in *The Green Man* starring the wonderful Alastair Sym where a car draws up outside a house in a vaguely familiar looking street in Turnham Green. In its day this shot was just a moment of continuity in the story, but to me watching fifty years later it has become a powerful image of social change, it's the only car in the road. Oh, to have lived then!

Going misty eyed about the past glosses over the realities of course. Just two words are enough to put me off anything pre-1900; dentistry and drains.

In our time the use of computers seems to be one of the most significant 'advances' that divides people. I am sure, as was William Morris in his day, that there will always be an interest in handmade things, including paintings, but for writing and research I could not manage without the humming beige box sitting on my desk. The ability to think onto the screen via a keyboard and then, by clicking

53°59.2'N 0°12.0'W

Soon to be mobile again?

a button, make instant text changes with a quick cut and paste is a wonderful thing. I would be lost as well without access to the internet. It is a good place to start when trying to find something on somewhere as small as Ulrome.

I found a *Driffield* website which has a *Yorkshire Wolds Villages Forum*, an electronic noticeboard where you can post messages hoping that someone might respond. I left the following:

I am working on a book about the places around Britain's coast that happen to fall at the 32 points of the compass. One of these is Ulrome and I am looking for any information on the place, no matter how obscure, bizarre, irrelevant or mundane it might seem.

I received a reply the same day:

"Obscure, bizarre, irrelevant or mundane. You have just summed up Ulrome in one sentence, can't wait to see the book!"

Now that's priceless. I would not have received that comment any other way and would not dare to describe somewhere in those terms myself.

Most of Ulrome is a few hundred metres back from the cliff top, a scattered collection of farms with

the downtown centre of the village dominated by a collection of modern red brick bungalows. The building that caught my attention was the unusual Methodist Church, a yellow engineering brick affair in a modest gothic style and looking somewhat reminiscent of a small, country railway station.

I'm now going back to the 1950s.

Desmond Rawson, who in 1949 founded Hornsea Pottery with his brother Colin, lived in Ulrome at the former Vicarage (Hornsea is five miles south of here). The tableware they produced, though not high art, were some of the classic designs that most represent for me the forward-looking 1950s style of ordinary everyday objects and are very collectible today. When in 1954 production was beginning to outgrow their Hornsea premises they installed a kiln in the coach house at the Ulrome Vicarage and went into production there for a couple of years making the black animal figures that are now some of their most sought after items.

So Ulrome has its place in history, even if it is only represented by a black streamlined polar bear.

When I started researching this location I thought

it was going to be for Ulrome only, hence my electronic message. However, after talking to the nice lady who is secretary to Skipsea Parish Council I discovered that although the rock on the beach on which I stood for my painting (I wanted to get the feeling of being surrounded by the incoming tide without getting too wet) was physically closer to Ulrome than to Skipsea, I was actually in Skipsea parish. The boundary takes an unusually irregular course across the countryside and meets the cliffs just north of the caravans that can be seen perched on the edge in my sketch.

Caravans seem to be one of the local farmers' biggest crops. The two villages appear to be united, or separated depending on your point of view, by hundreds of them. I counted nine caravan parks on my travels around the two parishes. At the height of the summer holidays you could no doubt add another zero to Ulrome's permanent population of 254.

Skipsea's houses outnumber Ulrome's people. On the village green there is a nineteenth century Reading Room where people could go to read the latest papers. Now the parish council meets there and so do the Skipsea History Workshop Group. I asked their secretary what they hoped to discover.

"Everything, we're going back as far as we can."

"You have a castle," I observed.

"It belonged to Drogo de Bevere who came over with William the Conqueror. There's only the mound and moat left, but when we've had floods it easier to see it all. We had some Second World War pill boxes once, but we've lost those because of the eroding cliffs."

I asked if she thought life had changed much, as it was obviously still a strong farming community.

"Pigs outnumber the people three to one. We found that there were a couple of windmills here,

and just south of the village there used to be a brick works. We have found their order books, you can see orders for bricks and tiles for buildings in the area. Quite a few people now work in servicing the caravan sites and there are people who commute to Hull and Beverley, York even. There are less people working these days, the population is quite elderly, they come here for holidays, like it and when they retire they sell up and move here."

I love researching the everyday lives of previous generations myself, the problem is knowing when to stop. How far do you go? I asked what they planned to do with all this information.

"We're creating a community archive and hope to publish some of it."

Can't wait to see the book. Now where have I heard that before?

The cliffs here seemed to disappear to infinity in both directions in a uniformly straight line without even deviating in height, just a long, straight red-ish brown wall. Their apparent unending-ness, to the north at least, in the direction of Bridlington and Flamborough Head was probably more an illusion than reality, as all the time I spent here the weather was persistently gloomy, with continuous fine rain mingled with copious amounts of spray off a typically grey North Sea reducing the visibility.

I stood alone, perched on my rock and gazed south through the spray. I remembered enough from my geography A-level course all those years ago to know that in this direction the cliffs actually do stretch to infinity, or they might just as well do so because I will be encountering them again at my next destination, Waxholme.

This time I found a way of painting them, but I wondered how I might tackle them a second time.

EAST BY SOUTH

WAXHOLME, WITHERNSEA
EAST RIDING OF YORKSHIRE

When I'm painting in the studio I use 5ml tubes of Winsor and Newton Artists' Watercolour and for sketching I use half pans, which are solid blocks of colour of about 16 x 11 x 8 mm.

For years I have used the same colours; cadmium yellow, yellow ochre, burnt umber, burnt sienna, alizarin crimson, cerulean blue, prussian blue and ivory black and have found that I can approximate everything that Mother Nature has to offer, or at least everything I have wanted to paint. Until now that is.

I have been beaten by the flower of the rapeseed plant.

If I had been a contemporary of William Morris, one of the followers of the Pre-Raphaelite Brotherhood maybe, I would not have had this problem as the crop was not grown in Britain for about 120 years, but in the 1950s the vivid yellow fields began to reappear and in late spring and early summer it seems like almost half the countryside is covered with the pungent plant.

Its dreadful smell can be put down to the fact that it's a first cousin to a cabbage, but at least we can be comforted by the fact that we may not have to be dazzled by its colour for ever. Because yellow reflects so much sunlight, rape does not absorb as much as it could for growth, so plant breeders are trying to breed it with green flowers instead. Sadly, there are no experiments under way to breed an odourless strain.

Bees, however, love it. Interestingly Waxholme means a homestead where wax from bees is produced. I know a farmer who grows rapeseed on boulder clay - "mans' land, not boys'" as he calls it - and he also keeps bees and makes honey. His early honey crop from the bees feeding mostly off his rapeseed sets very quickly and produces a whiter honey than later crops, but is just as tasty.

Lemon yellow nickel titanate, a pale acidic yellow solved my colour problem, mixed with my trusty cadmium yellow.

I started using watercolour in 1983 and some of my colours are still only into a second tube, so I would imagine that unless I become artist-in-residence to the Rapeseed Growers Association of Europe, archaeologists excavating the site of my studio in 20,000 years time are likely to unearth a fossilised but virtually complete tube of lemon yellow nickel titanate.

Holderness (the area between Flamborough Head and Spurn Head) is famous for its rapidly receding

53°44.4'N 0°01.1'E

coastline and on my visit the evidence was clear to see. I have already touched upon the possibility of falling off a cliff while working and the cliffs here looked more likely to fall away from under me than anywhere I have been before. I didn't like the look of the cracks that ran the length of the cliff top footpath here. This is a popular dog-walking route for Withernsea residents making the path well worn and distinct and here it clearly comes to an abrupt end.

You can see that the section of cliff that took the path round the edge of the field has fallen onto the beach below.

Holderness is the youngest natural area of English countryside. Until the end of the last ice age 10,000 years ago it did not exist. Glaciers deposited a layer of sand, stone and mud (boulder clay) to the east of the then coastline. This is the eastern edge of what we now call the Yorkshire and Lincolnshire

Withernsea lighthouse

Wolds and it has gradually been eroded back and shaped by the sea to form the present coast.

Undercutting of the soft cliffs by the sea is the main culprit, but rainfall filtering down through the ground and softening the clay is a contributory factor, making the area close to the cliff edge even less resistant to the sea's action.

At 116 locations along the coast the local authority monitors the rate of erosion, the average being two metres per year, but here it is only a third of that at 0.63 metre (about two feet). However, years could pass without any change and then several metres could disappear in one landslip. Since Roman times the Holderness coastline has retreated inland about three and a half miles and 30 villages have been lost, including Waxholme. All that bears the village's name now is the remains of a windmill, a farm and a few cliff top houses on the far side of the field of rapeseed.

The measuring method employed involves fixing a post in the ground and twice a year measuring the distance between the post and the cliff top. Dr Jon Mills, lecturer in Geomatics (the sciences and technologies involved in handling geographical data about the earth in digital form) at the University of Newcastle upon Tyne thinks this method "… relatively crude, making the provision of an up to date database of coastal change time consuming and inefficient."

Dr Mills is heading a team that's working to devise a more accurate and effective monitoring solution that will show the exact pattern of erosion, helping authorities to decide when and where to direct their resources.

"This will be achieved by creating a highly accurate 3D computer model which will illustrate the pattern of erosion and detail when it is most likely to occur and by how much."

There's something to make my insurance company happier, that's for sure.

Three types of readings are being used to create the computer model; small changes are recorded each month by satellite technology, then more detailed on-the-spot results are gained by using GPS (global positioning system) readings and digital aerial photographs taken from a microlight aircraft.

Withernsea is protected by a Victorian sea wall so in theory is safe, however storms in the winter of 1992/93 removed most of the beach fronting it and exposed the foundations. Cracks appeared in the wall and houses along the sea front experienced shock waves that could be measured on the earthquake measuring Richter scale. Eventually the cliffs to the north and south of the town will retreat leaving it exposed on its artificial headland.

It seems the town has suffered enough already. A friend of mine grew up in and around Withernsea and has seen it change over the last 50 years. I asked him how he felt about the town now.

"Very sad, very sad indeed. The average age is very high and unemployment is very high as well. It has been a depressed area for thirty years."

He can remember better times, though.

"There use to be a good community spirit. Music thrived, there used to be a light operatic society, church choirs and a good school choir, there was an annual performance of *Messiah*. In the summer lots of day trippers cycled out from east Hull. It was 17 miles or so but people would do that in those days because it's so flat, it wasn't too difficult for them."

I wondered if that meant it was not the place people went for a longer holiday even then.

"People used to come for a week from the West Riding mining areas and mill towns."

So what went wrong?

"We lost the railway in the Beeching cuts. People became more mobile and were taken with the possibilities of going somewhere else. Hull became depressed about that time too, that could not have helped."

It would seem to be a case of the railway giveth and the railway taketh away. The arrival of the Hull and Holderness Railway turned the quiet, off the beaten track farming village into a bustling holiday resort almost overnight. Now it's a quiet, off the beaten track holiday resort.

There is a view here reminiscent of that down Front Street in Tynemouth. Look down Pier Road towards the sea and at the end stands a building very much like the barbican and gatehouse of a great castle, but in this case it is all that remains of the long-gone pier, there's nothing behind it and it sums up Withernsea's plight quite well.

I am glad to say that the people here are not sitting back and letting their futures be washed away along with their cliffs. The Withernsea and South Holderness Regeneration Partnership, made up of organisations including local authorities and community groups are fighting to make improvements to the town, to engender a sense of pride and encourage local confidence again.

I have had first hand experience of just such an initiative, giving people the town they want by providing them with a voice in a forum that bypasses some of the usual systems of local control. It can take a long time to achieve its aims, with plenty of battles and fallings-out along the way, but the feeling of empowerment and pride and the great sense of achievement that results when you can see the new town rising from the rubble of the old one is overwhelming.

If my experience is anything to go by, look out; here comes Withernsea.

What needs to be focussed on in such a situation are the factors that make a town different, there is no point in trying to get what everywhere else has. I am not putting the following forward as a solution to the town's problems, it is just something that is different, unique in fact, and deserves a mention.

Withernsea has a lighthouse. I'll accept for a coastal town that is not unusual, but this one is half a mile inland, which is at least unconventional. I remember seeing it for the first time as I drove into the town from Waxholme, I knew exactly where the sea was as I had not long before been looking at it, so when I rounded a bend in the road and saw the lighthouse standing at the T-juction ahead I was so surprised I nearly drove into a builder's skip.

A light hasn't shone from its 39 metre high tower since 1976 and the building is now a museum. A museum in a lighthouse is hardly unique I hear you cry, but this one is a memorial to Kay Kendall, the Withernsea-born actress who starred alongside Kenneth More and Dina Sheridan in the 1953 film *Genevieve*. Now you have to admit, that *is* different.

EAST-SOUTH-EAST

NORTH END, MABLETHORPE
LINCOLNSHIRE

Alfred Tennyson, the Poet Laureate and later first Lord Tennyson was born not far inland at Somersby, where his father was Rector. His first published work (1827) was a joint venture with his brothers Charles and Frederick, a volume of poems for which they conceived the witty title *Poems by Two Brothers*. On publication day he came with Charles to Mablethorpe, where they sat among the dunes declaiming the verses to the empty sands … as you do.

The sands were empty when I was there. The vast beach and dunes to the north of the town are Mablethorpe's great assets, or should that be its saving grace?

I am conscious while making my visual record of these compass points that for the finished paintings I am occasionally turning my back on views that might be more representative of some of the locations. These visually unrecorded scenes sometimes provide the abiding impression I have of a place, but as a landscape painter I do not do ugly.

I do my best to find even in the grimmest of locations something that redeems it, something that says even here in this unattractive spot there is this, so it's not that bad really.

Perhaps that means I am not being completely objective and open minded and in the context of this book might give the impression that our coastline is more attractive than it really is, but I am not inventing anything. I only paint what is there, it just takes a bit of finding sometimes.

Fortunately I do not have to rely entirely on the paintings. Any imbalance can be redressed in my written view of each location. This is particularly relevant here where, for instance, in one of the town's more uplifting spots there is a holiday village surrounded by a tall perimeter fence topped with barbed wire. It brought to mind the film *The Great Escape* and I drove away humming the theme tune, hoping that I never get caught and hauled back there for more visual punishment. But the dunes and beach are great.

If you find yourself walking north away from the town along the sands (recommended) you may spot a harrier, or a falcon or even an eagle. Big cats: jaguar, puma and lynx are often seen here too, but I am not referring to the wildlife.

As well as being a nature reserve and the largest seal pupping area on the east coast, it is also what the RAF calls an Academic Range. That is, pilots fly their Jaguars, Falcons and Pumas etc to here, not just from

bases in Britain but also from Nato airfields all over Europe and even North America, to learn how to 'deliver ordnance' correctly. That doesn't mean how to wrap it properly and ensure it has the right value stamp on it, but it does involve making sure that it goes into the correct letterbox.

Sometimes they might be flying at over 6,000 metres with the letterbox obscured by cloud, in which case they have to rely on radar to locate the right front door. They are allowed to miss it by six metres, that's because the parcel they are delivering will obliterate the whole neighbourhood anyway as it thuds onto the doormat.

For some strange reason that other Poet Laureate, John Betjeman's line 'come friendly bombs and fall on Slough' suddenly springs to mind.

The range is crossed by a number of footpaths and rights of way and is not fenced off. Red flags are flown to warn of an exercise in progress. It also extends up to seven miles out to sea where there are floating targets. For some people the target practice is quite a spectacle and they come along with their picnics and folding chairs to spend the day watching.

The bombs, cannon shells and other ordnance are not live of course. The bombs are fitted with a small smoke charge to help locate them, for marking points out of ten for technical ability and artistic impression. At the end of an exercise a team clear the range of everything that was dropped or fired, so it's safe to take Gnasher for his evening walk.

The seals don't mind this mayhem in the slightest. As the Flight Sergeant in charge there explained to me,

"If it wasn't for the range they wouldn't be there."

The public are kept away for long periods of the day so they are left in 'peace' to enjoy what they like doing best, breeding and resting. No fishing is allowed in the offshore range (who would want to?) so there is plenty of food for them. The MOD even employ a warden to oversee the interaction between the public and the seals, as young of both species tend to get a little excited and the ones whose territory this is then go through a defence exercise of their own, with teeth.

Two nature reserves extend for nearly eleven miles along the coast northward from Mablethorpe (Saltfleetby–Theddlethorpe Dunes Reserve) to Grainthorpe Haven (Donna Nook Reserve), much of the area designated as Sites of Special Scientific Interest and some National Nature Reserve.

A variety of related habitats make up the reserves: sand bars, tidal sand and mudflats, sandy beach, ridges of dunes, salt and freshwater marshland and open lagoons, all a creation in one way or another of shifting sand.

The oldest landward dunes began to form on a storm beach in the thirteenth century and new dunes continue to be created in the area immediately to the north of Mablethorpe. The dunes and marshlands support an enormously varied bird population with over 250 species recorded. As the dunes system has developed areas of saltmarsh have become trapped between them. Over time their salinity decreases so changing the plant community that grows in them. In the summer the saltmarsh is particularly attractive in its covering of sea-lavender and there are extensive beds of samphire on the coastal fringe.

In some communities samphire seems to have undergone something of a rediscovery, or just discovery. Rick Stein, who can come and cook anything fishy in my kitchen any time he likes, reckons it's best blanched in fresh water, tossed in good olive oil with a squeeze of lemon juice and served warm. Nice!

53°20.8'N 0°15.8'E

Eric Drewery, who designed this book (as well as my previous two) grew up a few miles along the coast and remembers as a child picking samphire along these shores. My conversations with Eric usually revolve around supply dates for edited text, proof reading schedules, sizing of pictures and map content, but for once we talked about the subject in the text and he made his contribution there.

I asked him if there was a family samphire recipe.

"This goes back to when Mum used to be taken by her parents down to the coast on Thursday afternoons – it must have been in the 1920s or 30s, they picked samphire and dug for cockles. Grandfather was a baker and they were some of the first people in Grimsby to have a car – for deliveries, a 1914 Darraq. The samphire was washed and then steeped in malt vinegar and pickling spices for three to four days. It would then be transferred to clean vinegar and bottled.

It was used as an accompaniment to cold meats etc, usually haslet, chine or other dubious parts of the pig which used to be very popular in Lincolnshire."

I can identify with the unusual pork products. Where I live in Wiltshire there was a once famous bacon curing factory that boasted it used every part of the pig apart from its squeal. Older residents delight in telling of what became of the lesser thought of parts of the pigs anatomy and the delicious meals they made: Bath chaps, crispy fried chitterlings and stewed trotters for instance. Perhaps Ainsley, Nigela and Jamie would like to give those some thought.

Eric's mother, now in her 80s, still goes occasionally to various places around Mablethorpe for a swim in the sea. I asked her for a view of the area.

"Wonderful place, but we don't go into the town. The beach is lovely."

I'll agree with that.

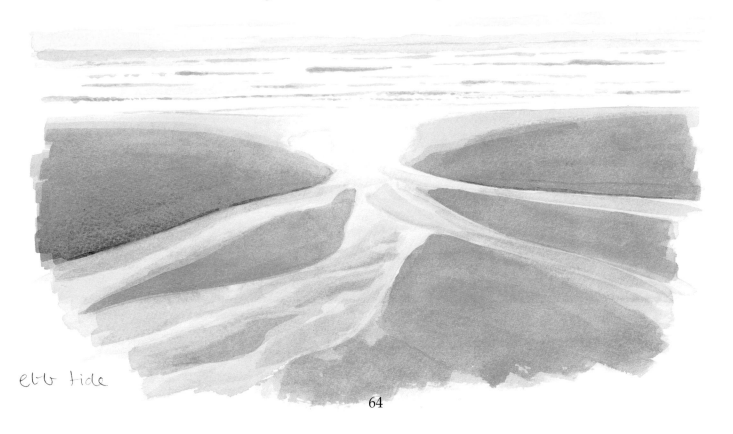

ebb tide

SOUTH-EAST BY EAST

SOUTHWOLD
SUFFOLK

I could begin by saying it is comforting to find that places like Southwold still exist on our coast, but I would be misleading you. Places like Southwold don't exist, but fortunately, Southwold does.

In Southwold a gentleman has the time, the space and the inclination to cycle slowly along the High Street, holding his handlebars with one hand and an open umbrella above his head with the other. It is also a place where no one gives him a second glance or thinks it an unusual sight. Southwold is the place where the car showroom still has a Morris Minor on display and where an attendant will still serve you at the filling station.

You might get the impression that the place has hardly changed in the last hundred years or so, but that is an illusion. It has kept up with everywhere else, but has managed to do so with dignity. It has held on to the essence of what makes Southwold special. That is partly due to what it lacks; modern housing estates, a marina, chain stores, clubs, amusement arcades, fairgrounds and candy floss.

Visitors seem to respect Southwold and attune to its singular charm. They keep it tidy, they do not make a lot of noise or drive fast, they are polite in shops and step off the pavement to let people pass.

They take their time, smile at passers by, pause to notice details of buildings. They become interested and return again and again.

Southwold is not pretty, but it is handsome. With the exception of the magnificent church, buildings are a mix of almost everything from Queen Anne onwards, but the similarity in scale, colour and materials from one to another has created a harmonious whole. Open spaces abound and it is these 'greens' that make the townscape so distinctive and marvellous and provide such a variety of vistas. They were created as firebreaks when the town had to be rebuilt after a disastrous fire in the seventeenth century destroyed mediaeval Southwold. So devastating was the event that it was the first time Parliament had declared anywhere in England a disaster area.

There is a sense of isolation. People do not 'pass through'. It is not on the route to somewhere else, there is one road in and it's a four mile journey off the A12. Sounds idyllic doesn't it? There are drawbacks.

There are 1,200 houses in Southwold and the permanent population is ... 1,200. How can that be? One third of the houses here are holiday homes.

I'm sorry if I whetted your appetite, but

unfortunately the place has already been discovered. I have some friends who grew up in nearby Lowestoft and they refer to Southwold as Fulham-by-the-Sea.

Property prices are already sky high and ordinary folk from round here can no longer afford them. The couple running the guest house where I stayed during my visit had two small children and I was told that there are only three other households with young children in the town. The primary school buses-in pupils from the surrounding villages.

If you are used to driving around in a certain amount of luxury; heated leather seats, walnut trim, climate control and names like Jaguar, Cadillac or Mercedes are your style, you may be interested to know that if you fancy a change of scene, for the same outlay you can buy yourself a Southwold beach hut.

Yes, I know it's only a glorified shed and names like Idleours, Chatterbox and Breakaway do not have that same ring of precision engineering and refinement about them, but you will have a place of your own by the sea. Well, until a storm washes it away that is, but at least you will still own the plot. I'm sure it wouldn't take long to knock together another one. You couldn't do that with a Lexus could you? There is a waiting list by the way, but there's only about a thousand people on it before you.

The town sits back from a low cliff, which has a substantial sea wall protecting its base. They haven't gone overboard in sea front development, in fact that part of town is relatively modest. The better and more interesting buildings and the Market Place seem to ignore it altogether. You stumble across the sea views almost by accident.

However, they do have a pier, but this one, as you might expect for Southwold, is different. For a start it's new. Apparently it's the first new one to be built in Britain for fifty years. There was one here before, but it had its share of accidents; storms, collisions, the usual peculiarly pier-like events and so in 1998 it closed. The following year the owners took the brave decision to build a new one.

As well as providing above-the-sea refreshments, with a particularly splendid view south along the beach, there is a water powered clock, an exhibition about piers and seaside holidays, a shop and a room of amusements intriguingly labelled The International Bureau of Stimulation and Assessment, where, entirely by machine, you can unravel the secrets of your DNA, let the chiropodist give your foot a treat, immerse yourself in a total eclipse, witness an extraordinary rodent experiment and take home a prescription for all your medical problems.

For some, Southwold means the town's major employer Adnam's, the brewery that cloaks down-wind parts of the town in the distinctively delicious smell of hops cooking and, to the delight of organic gardeners, makes its local deliveries with a horse drawn dray. For others it will be memorable for its individual shops, the quality of its food, the late Victorian lighthouse, like that at Withernsea surrounded by houses, or for the fifteenth century knapped-flint St Edmunds, reckoned to be the finest coastal church in England.

The interior is light and hung with fishermens' nets, there is a glorious painted screen, a painted and gilded hammer-beam roof and, as old as the building itself, the unusual Southwold Jack, a half life-size figure in military uniform, which, with a pull on a rope can be made to strike a bell with his axe to signal the start of a service.

52°19.2'N 1°41.6'E

Fishermen's Sheds, Blackshore

I had been to Southwold before, in the mid 1980s when I visited nearby Walberswick on a Charles Rennie Mackintosh pilgrimage and it was just as I remembered it, but on this second occasion I discovered something I had not seen before that made this visit even more memorable.

At the southern end of the town, where its early nineteenth century gentrification is most evident and where the coast is guarded by a row of six Elizabethan guns, Ferry Road shelters behind a line of dunes for about half a mile before reaching the point at which the River Blyth enters the sea. The road turns and runs inland along the north bank of the river, becoming a track, Blackshore.

Blackshore is Southwold's harbour and looks like it was constructed as a film set for David Copperfield. A series of pontoons built out from the shore provide moorings for Southwold's small fishing fleet. Nets, floats, buoys, ropes, crab and lobster pots are all stacked on the ground, or hung over, or from, the pontoons and boats.

On the landward side of Blackshore there's a long line of wooden buildings; sheds, huts and barns of all shapes and sizes, but all of them black. From some you can buy fish fresh off the boat and from one even cooked fish fried in batter the traditional way. There is also a chandlers, a boat building and repair yard, Southwold Sailing Club and even a pub, which apparently provides the best hangovers in town. The ensemble is a visual treat as refreshing as a pint of Adnams.

Southwold town is a delight, there is an air of peace and decorum that makes a welcome change, but after a couple of days of its elevated allure the straight forward, down to earth nature of the harbour comes as something of a relief. It's the balance that provides reassuring proof, should you need it, that Southwold does live in the real world after all.

SOUTH-EAST

CLACTON-ON-SEA
ESSEX

The coastline in the vicinity of Clacton is most inviting, offering over eight miles of sheltered beaches and an easy three days march to London.

That's not what you might expect to find in the average holiday brochure. In fact that conclusion, drawn before Clacton-on-Sea had even been invented, was made by the Board of Ordnance in 1794, after the coast had been surveyed amid fears of an invasion from France. As a result four Martello towers were built around here.

When the invaders eventually arrived 77 years later, led by the *Queen of the Orwell*, a Woolwich Steam Packet Company paddle steamer en route from London to Ipswich, the new resort of Clacton-on-Sea's first structure, the pier, had been built to welcome them ashore.

Before that there was little more than the small village of Great Clacton just a mile inland with Little Clacton nearby, an estate belonging to St Paul's Cathedral and farmland. The cliff tops were inhabited by corn fields and the coast was considered so unhealthy that the Martello towers' garrison were quartered five miles inland at Weeley.

The first recorded attempt at enticing people down to the beach came in 1824 when the *Ship Inn* in

Great Clacton advertised a bathing machine for hire.

Something more grand was planned when fifty acres of farmland, Sea Side House Farm, was bought in 1865 by engineer and entrepreneur Peter Bruff, who at that time was building the Colchester to Walton-on-the-Naze railway.

His idea was to lay a new branch line with a station close to the cliffs at Clacton, build a pier to enable the already-established east coast paddle steamer trade to bring visitors ashore and develop a new resort 'being entirely a new creation and not the adoption of an existing town, none of the evils inseparable from old watering places will be allowed to exist in it. There will be no slums, nor any object that can offend the eye.'

I went to Clacton knowing little and anticipating less, but somehow assuming my eye would be offended. I don't know why that should be. Perhaps the town suffers from having a name that does not elevate one's expectations. Maybe, despite such lovely places as Burnham-on-Crouch and Maldon and having lived in the county myself for two years, the anti-Essex propaganda had claimed another victim. I've never thought of William Morris or Chris Beetles as fitting the stereotype of 'Essex man', so

why did I assume Clacton would be the ghastly Southend mark two?

I was therefore greatly and pleasantly surprised by what I saw as I drove around the town and along the sea front. 'Sunny Clacton' lived up to its billing. It might have been early October on the calendar – and the place I had lunch at had, disturbingly, a Christmas tree decorating one corner of the room – but in the warm, sun-roof-open sunshine of a clear blue sky, with Jonathan Agnew's commentary on the England versus Zimbabwe cricket coming out of the car radio, it was July in my mind.

Clacton is a clean and pleasant land. The town's motto *Lux, Salubritas, Felicitas* or Light, Health, Happiness might have been an ambition in 1871, but is still appropriate today. Modern Clacton is, on the whole, residential with a smattering of industrial estates and generally well endowed with facilities for its size.

The town is not exactly overflowing with hotels, the last one to be built was the art deco Oulton in 1936, now altered and converted into flats, suggesting that Clacton's days as a major holiday destination may just have passed their peak. As a place to go for a day away from London however, it is ideal for those looking for something that falls both geographically and culturally somewhere between Southwold and Southend.

At sea level there is a seven mile long sea wall. Here you can walk for hours below the low, formal gardens planted on the face of the sloping cliffs and away from the traffic on Marine Parade, all the way eastward as far as Walton-on-the-Naze, if your fancy takes you.

In the opposite direction the cliffs gradually loose what stature they had and at Clacton Wash this natural barrier disappears altogether, with two Martello towers guarding the potential landing site.

In 1937 the land around the first of these towers became the site of a pioneering social experiment, the second Butlins holiday camp. The idea did not go down too well in Clacton at the time. The fact that the camp was to be self contained led to concern that the town would not gain any extra business by it, the local hoteliers and boarding house keepers assumed it would take some of their trade away and it was thought that it might lower the tone of the area.

Billy Butlin won the doubters over by taking them to Skegness, the site of his first camp, so they could see the beneficial effects it had there.

The opening of the Clacton site more or less coincided with Parliament passing the 'Holidays with pay Act' and Butlins' success lay in their ability to provide families with a holiday that could be paid for with their newly acquired entitlement.

Butlins' entertainment programme gave many well-known performers a first public stage on which to hone their talents. Clacton's happy campers of 1958 for instance would have had Roy Hudd as one of their red-coated helpers and on the evening's bill at the *Pig and Whistle* bar was a seventeen years old Cliff Richard. Hi-de-hi!

The notion of 'holiday' (and 'camp') has changed greatly since then of course and consequently the Clacton Butlins closed in 1983.

The site has been developed into a sadly typical housing estate that gives the impression, unlike its predecessor, that no time was wasted in thinking too deeply about what should be put there. If Peter Bruff could see this he would not be a happy man.

At one corner of the site, on a prime sea front

51°46.5'N 1°07.2'E

Waverley arriving at Clacton Pier

location, is a three-storey block with a completely blank gable end facing the sea, there's not a single window in it to take advantage of the wonderful views. In my opinion that is unforgivable.

I contacted the planning office at Tendring District Council to find out if there was some strange regulation that created this aberration. The very helpful planning officer, who was so overworked he was still at his desk at 7pm, was most aggrieved that no regulation could be found to prevent it from happening, but added that they would look very favourably on any plans to knock a window through

and suggested that a balcony or two would look even better.

The developers dealt with the site from their regional office in Dartford (out of sight …?). One employee I spoke to remembers visiting the site, just once, on a wet and windy day and wondered if weatherproofing might have been the reason. That was such a lame excuse I had to consider naming and shaming them.

Just by the second Martello tower is a rock breakwater, which has created a small, gloriously sandy bay in which a couple of inshore fishing boats were moored. It could almost have been Martella, Corsica rather than Martello, Clacton.

A fortunate conjunction of tide, sun and appropriate footwear coaxed me out into the calm shallows at this point. Looking back, with the water washing around my feet and up the beach, a flash of inspiration struck and I saw the finished Clacton painting staring back at me. Sometimes I'm not always that sure what will be my chosen image and time, even a month or two, can be required to filter out the less significant moments of a visit, but on this occasion it came in one sudden rush of *Lux, Salubritas et Felicitas.*

Before leaving I felt I ought to investigate the pier, as it was where the Clacton-on-Sea story began. I wandered out to the very end, took in the panorama of the town's sea front, stared out to sea for a while, then something most peculiar and dream-like happened.

There was a boat making its way eastward along the coast a couple of miles or so offshore, an unusual looking vessel, but difficult to make out at that distance. It was too big to be a fishing boat and much too small to be a cargo vessel. As it drew closer I could see that it had a central funnel, or even two, raked back possibly. Closer still it appeared that the wake was coming from somewhere amidships, like it would have done from … a paddle steamer. In fact, it was soon plain to see that it was a paddle steamer and I realised it had to be the *Waverley*, the only one I knew of still in regular use around Britain's coast, built, like the *Queen of the Orwell*, on the Clyde.

Its course changed, I thought at first just to get closer inshore, I then stood in disbelief as it became clear it was coming alongside the pier to tie up. I was experiencing that day back in July 1871 when it all started. How is that for being in the right place at the right time?

SOUTH-EAST BY SOUTH

DUNGENESS
KENT

If you cannot remember whether you have been to Dungeness or not, take it from me you haven't been; you would definitely remember it.

I arrived in the area after spending several hours behind the wheel of my car driving through heavy rain. It was the sort of day when you seem to be in a permanent twilight state, quite appropriate as it turns out.

I had decided to stay overnight in the nearby town of Rye, having been told that it was a bit special. I was reminded of that old Ronnie Barker sketch in which he posed as a television weather presenter. It went something like "… tomorrow it will be cool in Goole, dry in Rye and if you live in Lissingdown (pause for the punch-line and anticipatory laughter) we suggest you take an umbrella with you."

Rye is an historic and picturesque hilltop town and is everything you imagine a mediaeval town to be; it's a real gem. The narrow, winding and cobbled streets lined with beautiful timber-framed buildings and its elevated setting above the flat surrounding countryside make it a very special place indeed.

Having sorted out somewhere to stay I announced that I was off to Dungeness for the evening. Maybe it was my imagination, but at the mention of Dungeness I'm sure everyone present took a step back and became a little twitchy. Did the lights flicker just then and was that noise outside thunder or just an empty truck rumbling by?

"Dungeness," they murmured. "Some people here call that the twilight zone."

I wasn't quite sure whether that was a warning or just a general piece of local information, but it was not the reaction I had when I told some friends who knew the place that I was off there. They went into a positive swoon.

"Ooh! Dungeness, do you want someone to carry your bags?" was their response.

From Rye, the road to Dungeness passes through the coastal village of Camber, noted for its huge dunes, a holiday camp and the fact that it features in the book *Boring Postcards*.

Next is the small town of Lydd. This is probably not the place to say much about Lydd, but the fact that the town has an explosive named after it, Lyddite, must be unique.

Beyond Lydd lies Dungeness.

Covering an area of 30 square miles, Dungeness is the largest area of shingle in Europe and, in the rest of the world, only Cape Canaveral in Florida is

50°54.4'N 0°58.3'E

larger. The shingle is flint from the chalk beds under the Channel and has been accumulating here for well over five thousand years, building out from Romney Marsh in a series of more than six hundred ridges, which have now formed a promontory, Dungeness Point. In effect it is a gigantic triangular beach.

Every year, mostly during the winter months, about 100,000 cubic metres of the shingle is moved by the sea from west to east around the Point, removing some material from the south shore and slowly extending the east shore.

Dungeness is an 'I've never seen anything like it' sort of place that evokes a definite response. As a natural feature it is extraordinary enough, but what makes it incredible is man's development of the site.

There is an otherworldly atmosphere, where you need to forget all your normal responses to the built and natural environments. Dungeness is inconceivable and incomparable.

The most obvious features of the site as one crosses the shingle wilderness from Lydd are the nuclear power stations. These are products of the 'bleak functionalism' school of architecture and are probably at their best when sea fog reduces visibility to less than the distance between the buildings and the site's perimeter fence. They are neither the most

Downtown Dungeness

interesting nor the most unusual here, but they do add a certain *je ne sais quoi* to the atmosphere.

If you feel so inclined you can take a guided tour round Dungeness A, the old mid 1960s Magnox station. I did and would recommend it. Whatever your views on nuclear energy you will come away enriched.

To protect the power stations from erosion, shingle is removed from the east shore and transported by lorry to the south shore where it is deposited on the beach, thus effectively halting the natural movement of material. If this is the only recycling British Nuclear Fuels Limited are interested in we have nothing to be concerned about.

Trinity House's contribution to the landscape is also substantial. Standing close to the power stations is the old Dungeness lighthouse, made redundant when the construction of the former made its light invisible from the west. As neighbours it has some late nineteenth century light keepers' houses and an unusual round building that was once the keepers' accommodation at the base of its 1792 predecessor.

A few hundred metres to the east of this group stands the latest lighthouse. At 140 metres it is Trinity House's tallest and, measuring only 3.7 metres in diameter, its slender tower has a space rocket appearance that adds a nice Cape Canaveral allusion to the scene.

Even the two and a half lighthouses and the power stations together are still not enough to steal the show from the buildings that give Dungeness its individuality. These are the homes of the Dungeness residents, but it's not just the buildings themselves that give the place its strange quality. The plot of land each occupies, how the buildings relate to each other and to the one strip of tarmac that crosses the shingle all add to the atmosphere.

I hesitate to refer to them as houses, although that is what they are. They do not conform to the norm, but they are at least individualistic, some with great charm and more often than not verging on the rustic.

They do not appear to have been positioned according to an overall plan and the lack of a defined boundary between each one and the almost non-existent gardens creates a temporary, even frontier town look. If they had wheels the place would have a nomadic encampment feel to it. Indeed that is close to the origin of many of these buildings, for in most cases they started life as railway carriages.

The only similarity between this and Rye is that the buildings are made of wood.

By the time I arrived the rain had ceased and I wandered around in a cold, damp March breeze and the evening's gloom, trying to identify possible locations for the next day's work.

Eventually I retired to the warmth of *The Pilot*, the 'local' that was, I had been advised, an experience I should not miss. I was met by the silence of a room full of people earnestly involved in the consumption of seriously laden plates of fish and chips and mushy peas (portions are offered as normal or large). It is what *The Pilot* is famous for and clearly why the clientele had come on this particular night. By nine o'clock when most pubs are beginning to fill they had all gone home and I had the staff to myself.

We chatted for a while about life here. It was interesting to hear them say they lived "on" Dungeness, as if they were islanders. I could understand why, there is that feeling of separateness and their outlook and way of life is clearly different. There is a Bohemian spirit here, which you rarely find in Britain today.

The next day arrived with the continuation of the gloomy light, but by the time the forecast rain arrived I was a guest of BNFL, discovering how green nuclear power is and how dangerously radioactive old wristwatches with luminous dials are.

The lack of fences and conventionally cultivated gardens gives the impression that Dungeness is open for all to roam freely, but that is not the case. Property boundaries are not permitted and although the English Nature (some of it is a National Nature Reserve) notice boards indicate that 600 different plants grow in the shingle, out of season it's difficult to imagine that there are as many as 600 plants on the entire headland.

Grass grows in patches where the shingle is more stable, but as the importation of soil is not allowed those who want to have something they can call a garden often turn to tubs and pots. Some, in that free-thinking Dungeness spirit, find less conventional means to create a garden, like a carefully placed collection of redundant marker buoys, a mountain of plastic sandals tied together, or a thoughtfully planted border of old brushes.

Dungeness is a private estate. Until 1840 it was a wild corner of Kent with just a few Napoleonic era gun batteries. Then there was a plan to turn it into a port for ocean going liners. The Southern Railway bought the land and built a line there but the port didn't materialise. The railway carriages were never used and were taken off the track and eventually turned into houses.

The estate passed through a number of private owners until bought by Gordon Payne. He was an engineer and one time Mayor of Lydd who had worked on Dungeness and had fallen in love with the place. To give the tenants more security – until then their leases came up for renewal quarterly – he arranged for those that wanted to, to buy their properties and put the rest on more secure long term leases, turning the estate into a trust in 1964.

His action was not entirely altruistic though. He was also of the opinion that "One day someone's going to want all these pebbles".

To preserve its unique character the local planning authority apply special measures that strictly control any alterations or modifications. This for instance includes the colour of roofs and doors and the ban on fences.

Barring a Chernobyl-like incident, it would seem that only Mother Nature has the power to make any major changes to this wonderfully idiosyncratic spot, the gravel drive of the Garden of England.

SOUTH-SOUTH-EAST

GORING-BY-SEA
WEST SUSSEX

There is something peculiarly English about our suburbs and the nearer you get to London the more prevalent that style of building and urban planning becomes.

Those cosy, semi-rural avenues lined with flowering cherry trees and rows of houses with all the architectural details that doff their caps to our vernacular heritage; rustic brick, stone mullions, sweeping two storey Cotswold gables over tile-hung bays, deep overhanging eaves, projecting exposed timbers, oriels over Gothic Revival porches, small paned Queen Anne windows, Jacobean leaded lights, white panelled doors with stained glass images of sunrays and galleons, a splattering of pebbledash.

It is not quite anywhere in particular. A hint of Suffolk here and a bit of Shropshire there, with some nice Sussex weatherboarding and each one almost a mirror image of its neighbour. Some crazy paving, a square of lawn, a hydrangea, a privet hedge and a rustic arch with a rose or maybe some honeysuckle growing over. A green and pleasant land just a short walk from the shops and the station. It's enough to have Sir Edwin and Gertrude turning in their graves.

No, I'm not mocking it. In its own peculiar way this stylistic mish-mash has somehow taken on a life of its own and in a strange sort of way I've come to appreciate some aspects of it (oh dear, I'll be wearing Hush Puppies and drinking Horlicks next). I'll let you into a little secret, I was born in just such a house. I call the style North Circular Tudor, but it could have been very different, more Autobahn Moderne.

When it was a new idea in the hands of C. F. A. Voysey and Ebenezer Howard it was much admired and taken abroad by Hermann Muthesius, the cultural attaché at the German Embassy in London who published *Das Englische Haus* in Berlin 1904/5.

The ideas therein came back within 25 years like something from outer space as the stunning *New Ways*, a compact white concrete cube in Northampton by Peter Behrens, who had Walter Gropius, Le Corbusier and Mies van der Rohe working in his Berlin office at various times. Imagine what our suburbs would look like now if our own architects and planners had found the same inspiration in those ideas developing here at the end of the nineteenth century.

Goring-by-Sea is a suburb; the western suburb of Worthing. When compared with other south coast towns Worthing stands out as being pretty good and as suburbs go generally Goring is very good indeed, a superb suburb.

If Southwold is Fulham-by-the-sea and Brighton London-by-the-sea, then Goring is closer to being more of a Hampstead-by-the-sea. It's not quite that good, but it's impressively okay all the same.

Spacious and green, Goring is more up-market than the average suburb, there is more individuality and variety, with more architectural integrity. There is often a refined simplicity, a streamlining of one period or style, which adopts the principles of the past without slavishly copying anything, producing something completely original, individual and fresh.

There are some good examples of suntrap houses with their curved glazing and some superb International Style post-*New Ways* white cubes. Roads, verges and pavements are wide, houses set well back and substantial trees grow everywhere.

Modern developers have something to learn from Goring. Sadly, too many of them these days can only manage an unimaginative regurgitating of their predecessors' mistakes, with no reference to local styles, materials or conditions and no sense of the times in which they are built. The only consideration seems to be profit and to hell with the quality of materials and of the environments they are creating.

As Lucinda Lambton so forcefully expressed it "a pestilential pox has swept across the land".

The name Goring-by-Sea arrived with the railway in 1906, to distinguish it from the Oxfordshire Goring. Some signs of the pre-suburb days survive in the occasional old building, a row of farm cottages and the four grand houses, the grounds of which supplied the building land for the development from the mid 1930s onwards.

Through the grounds of one, Goring Hall, runs Goring's great landmark. A magnificent mile-long avenue of one hundred and fifty year old Holm oaks, Ilex Avenue, with three other avenues branching off it, and running down to the sea front, providing a green lung through the houses and linking the countryside with the sea.

Thankfully the sea front is not a gaudy development of hotels, blocks of flats and amusement arcades, just quiet, human-scale houses.

Between these and the beach lies a broad expanse of grassland beside which Marine Crescent and Marine Drive form a link between the village of Ferring to the west and Worthing immediately to the east. This open space seems to indicate a refined attitude toward the beach and the sea. 'We know it's there and we will enjoy it from time to time, but we would not wish to do anything so vulgar as look at it from our property.'

A line of tamarisk bushes marks the boundary between the open grassland and the beach, where a number of small fishing boats will also be found and where it is possible, if you are there at the right time, to buy fish direct from the fishermen. Plaice, cod and huss are the most likely catches.

However, not everything in the garden is rosy. Close to Marine Drive and Marine Crescent some of the houses are below sea level and if a south-westerly gale coincides with a high spring tide the Environment Agency delivers sand bags to the houses most at risk from flooding.

I noticed that the groynes (or breakwaters) here are particularly splendid, in unusually good condition, so I spoke to Worthing Borough Council's Chief Engineer to find out more about them and the need for beach protection here.

The bay between Selsey Bill and Beachy Head is a discrete sediment cell, so what is there is likely to stay

50°48.2'N 0°25.7'W

Fishing boat with 'The Plantation' avenue

there naturally. The Council's policy is 'hold the line'. They are trying desperately not to tamper with nature, but have to trick it into keeping in place as much material as they can to give themselves maximum protection from the sea, hence the need for the groynes.

Worthing's are made of Douglas Fir. They take quite a pounding from the sea particularly in winter, and the movement of beach material across them scours away the timber necessitating their replacement about every fifteen years. A new type of groyne made out of Mendip rocks has been designed. Each rock weighs between two and a half and six tonnes, and to date three timber ones have been replaced with these new affairs. These should last fifty years and overall work out cheaper than the traditional ones.

So these wooden constructions we have become so used to may one day be a thing of the past. Where there is still considered to be a need to continue protecting beaches in this way Mendip rock could be the way ahead. Like *New Ways* we have new ways, much like the Moderne white cube, these chunks of limestone imported from Somerset might at first be a visual shock, but in time will no doubt become as accepted a 'natural' feature of Goring's townscape as Ilex Avenue.

You're going to hate me for this, but I'm afraid I am going to use the 's' word again. You can turn over to the Isle of Wight now if you like for all those lovely chalk cliffs and more about that nice poet from Lincolnshire, but it'll be your loss; honest.

If you are still with me brace yourself. I will break it to you gently, then when you have recovered we can go off together and wallow in it for a few more paragraphs. Are you ready? Shingle. There, that wasn't so bad was it?

This is going to come as a great disappointment to the bucket and spade brigade, but we are privileged to have been blessed with so much of it and must cherish every last tiny sea-washed flinty piece. Why is this? Well, believe it or not, beaches of vegetated shingle – that is shingle identified as such at the surface on geological maps – are a very rare phenomenon world wide, occurring in North-West Europe – mostly in Britain and some in Scandinavia, New Zealand and Japan.

Very little research into shingle habitats has been done. Most of what we know today comes from research by the University of East Anglia, funded by BNFL after so much damage was done to the shingle at Dungeness by the construction of the power stations.

The study of shingle as a natural habitat is considered to be so important by the various levels of local government here that they employ, with the help of English Nature, local harbour authorities and conservation groups, a Vegetated Shingle Officer, who is based in an office in nearby Bognor Regis Town Hall. I took a trip over there to see what her work was all about.

The major role of the West Sussex Vegetated Shingle Project is to increase public awareness and understanding of the habitat, to be a shingle evangelist. The hope is that this will help to prevent exploitation and damage in the future.

This one-woman show requires someone who can perform a wide variety of tasks. The work involves conducting surveys of the habitat, producing interpretive material for specific sites, negotiating for (and advising on) restoration projects, fundraising, going into schools to talk to teachers and pupils, giving presentations to local communities and more. You need to be a botanist, a marine scientist, a photographer, an exhibition designer, a lobbyist, a school teacher, a broadcaster, a fundraiser, a writer, a public speaker, a publicist … above all, enthusiastic and waterproof. You can see that I was impressed.

Shingle by the way, just in case you have come this far and still want a more precise definition, is an accumulation of pebbles ranging from 2 to 200mm diameter. It doesn't sound half so interesting when you express it in such dry terms does it?

SOUTH BY EAST

TENNYSON DOWN
ISLE OF WIGHT

Of all English landscapes the one I love the most is chalk downland, particularly that of my adopted county, Wiltshire. So to leave behind those beautiful and inspiring hills to visit more downs, this time with the bonus of a sea view, is sublime.

The narrow ridge of chalk that crosses the Isle of Wight in an east-west alignment passes barely noticed across much of the island. On Wight's western side, however, immediately to the west of its most public emergence as the low cliffs around Freshwater Bay, a three miles long ridge rises majestically like a whale's back, eventually falling away in a picturesque staccato of stacks aligned behind the Needles lighthouse off the island's western tip.

Off the narrow road from Freshwater Bay to Alum Bay that runs roughly parallel with this ridge a lane climbs, gently at first, to a National Trust car park in a disused chalk pit at the base of the escarpment.

A well signed footpath skirts the edge of the pit and takes you in the shelter of the ridge to Freshwater Bay in one direction and in the other eventually over open downland to the coastguard cottages above the Needles. It is an easy path that saves much of its drama for the views at either end.

From this spot there is also another much more challenging path that allows you to climb up the escarpment and onto the highest part of the ridge.

Walking on chalk downland can often be more difficult than it looks. The gently rounded hills look inviting, but so often their lack of ruggedness belies their scale and a seemingly casual stroll can turn into an exhausting test of stamina. Going straight up the side of an escarpment is not to be recommended, but here the existence of a path suggests that it must not be too arduous.

This steep path climbs up the surprisingly thickly wooded north facing hillside, turning occasionally and for much of the way stepped to make the task slightly less taxing. Eventually an end to the sheltered tunnel through the tangle of branches comes into view and you emerge breathless onto a wide-open space of short grass characteristic of chalk downland, with a view of the English Channel beyond.

One hundred and forty seven metres above sea level, fifty per cent higher than the chalk cliffs at Dover and not far short of Beachy Head, this used to be known as High Down, but now it is Tennyson Down.

50°39.9'N 1°32.4'W

The Tennysons, Alfred who was made Poet Laureate on the death of Wordsworth, his wife Emily whom he married that same year in 1850, and their baby son Hallam had been living in Twickenham. They wanted to escape from London to somewhere more secluded in attractive surroundings. In those days there was probably nowhere more accessibly isolated than the Isle of Wight and it is said that one November evening Alfred and Emily rowed across the Solent under 'a daffodil sky' and found Farringford, the late eighteenth century castellated gothic house that was to become their home for thirty nine years.

Farringford, now a hotel, sits in wooded parkland between High (Tennyson) Down and the Freshwater to Alum road, with views out northward across the Solent to the New Forest and of the English Channel seen to the south-east through the break in the chalk ridge at Freshwater Bay, now a view mostly obscured by trees.

To the east, through the drawing room windows is a view across Afton Down, a location that will be re-membered by some, who may subscribe to a different definition of poetry, as that of the 1970 Isle of Wight Pop Festival, where Jimi Hendrix performed in public in Britain for the last time, 18 days before his death.

Tennyson described Farringford's location as 'close to the ridge of a noble down' and it was his custom to take a daily walk on the down. Farringford sits on the 35 metre contour line of a modern OS map, so his walk, if he went only as far as the high point of the down where a memorial to him now stands, was of about a mile in each direction, climbing through 112 metres. Accounts by friends who occasionally accompanied him suggest that more often than not this walk took him as far as the Needles, a round trip of about six miles.

From the down the views are magnificent. In good visibility the chalk downs of Dorset, Wiltshire and Hampshire more than 30 miles away can be seen. Closer, from the west clockwise there is Swanage on its limestone hills, the chalk cliffs – a westward extension of this ridge – of Ballard Down, Poole Harbour and the buildings of Poole and Bournemouth, Hengitsbury Head and Christchurch, the New Forest and west Solent with the ferries crossing from Lymington to Yarmouth, Southampton, the western half of Wight with the hills to the north of St Catherine's Point rising to 237 metres and finally to the south the English Channel.

Tennyson's monument is a tall granite Celtic cross erected in 1897 and maintained by Trinity House as a sea mark. On one side is carved *Tennyson Born August 6 1809 Died October 6 1892*, on the other *In memory of Alfred Lord Tennyson this cross is raised a beacon to sailors by the people of Freshwater and other friends in England and America.*

Hallam, the second Lord Tennyson donated Tennyson Down to the National Trust in 1927 in memory of his father. More land in the vicinity, including West High Down, the Needles headland and Headon Warren, a golden sandstone ridge just to the north, has more recently been acquired by the Trust by private gifts, grants from the Countryside Commission and purchases with Neptune funds.

The north face of the down, sheltered from the prevailing wind, has grown its covering of woodland since the 1950s when grazing ceased. The Trust is now clearing some areas to create patches of grassland and encourage more varied wildlife. Recently a small herd of short horn cattle was reintroduced to help manage the grassland by preventing the woody plants from spreading back

Tennyson monument

into the cleared areas. In prehistoric times all of the down was probably covered in woodland, being cleared for grazing by stone-age farmers.

On my first visit, a cool and cloudy mid-September afternoon, I took a stroll out toward the Needles and found myself walking through an area where acid-loving plants more usually associated with heathland – heathers and gorse, were growing freely on the alkaline chalk alongside the more usual downland plants.

Occasionally a pair of serious walkers would pass by, sometimes accompanied by a healthy looking

canine companion. One couple perched themselves on a bench by the memorial and through their binoculars were sure they could see land to the south. This could only be the Cherbourg peninsula, but I was sure it was nothing more than a large ship passing up the Channel in the sea-lane on the French side.

Through my binoculars I spotted an inshore fishing boat not far offshore, this appeared as a tiny speck when viewed with the naked eye and brought home to me the scale of the cliffs I was standing on. From my position the metre or so between me and the cliff edge felt a comfortable distance, but if anyone 147 metres away down there saw me, I'm sure they would not have held to that opinion.

A few weak shafts of sunlight broke through the blanket of cloud to illuminate the calm sea between the Needles and Swanage, creating pools of silvery brilliance in an otherwise overcast scene.

I used this first visit to familiarise myself with the down, identify a few locations that may respond well to some early morning sunshine should that transpire the next day and made some notes about the locale.

Fortunately the following morning provided the predicted weather and after a filling breakfast I almost ran, as much as that is possible, up the steep path onto the down in my eagerness to get there, arriving gasping for breath in the sunshine. The light and shade had become reversed since yesterday. A blue sea sparkled in the sunlight and was broken only by the occasional purple/grey shadow of a passing cloud. The chalk cliffs looked stunning; bliss! Oh, to have this just an energetic walk away from home ...

SOUTH TO WEST

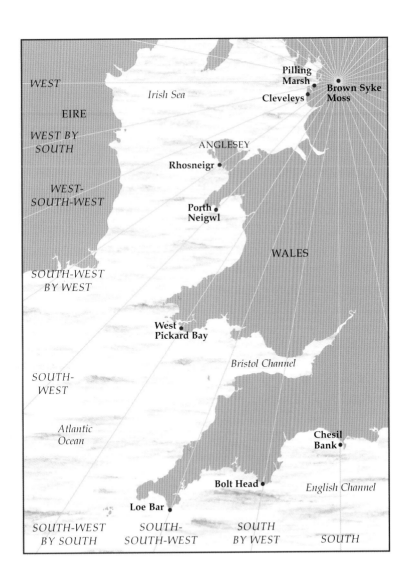

SOUTH

CHESIL BANK
DORSET

Some time ago I started to make a list of what I considered to be the natural wonders of Britain, thinking that one day I might get round to painting and writing about them for a book. Though occasionally added to it is still just a list, but Chesil Bank was my first entry so at least I have made a start, albeit in a different context.

Chesil Bank, taking its name from *cisel* an Old English word for shingle, is a beach with a difference. You will find it variously described as a bank, a beach, a bar, or even a spit. On the Ordnance Survey maps it is named Chesil Beach. Off the road from Weymouth to Portland, which runs beside it, is the Chesil Beach Visitor Centre, where there is the office of the warden in charge of the Chesil Bank and the Fleet Nature Reserve.

Whatever it is called, as it links the otherwise Isle of Portland with the rest of Dorset it is in fact a tombolo (not to be confused with tombola, a prize draw made from a revolving drum, or Tom Bowler, the winner of the 1997 Carnegie Medal for children's books). If you live locally you might refer to it simply as 'the Chesil'.

As tombolos go, Chesil is world class. Instead of linking Portland with Dorset the easy way by spanning the mere one and a half miles between the two, it swaggers all the way to Abbotsbury, ten miles away to the north-west, before it deigns to join the rest of Britain. It then continues for another eight miles to West Bay, where it begins to look almost like a conventional shingle beach, coming to an end where the River Brit enters the sea.

At eighteen miles in total, I suppose it was almost inevitable that one of my compass points would fall somewhere along its length. I'm so glad it did.

None of this, however, gives any impression of Chesil's immense size. To call it a beach is like referring to the Grand Canyon as a bit of a gorge.

Generally it is 150 to 200 metres wide and rises to 14 metres in height at the Portland end. If you find that difficult to imagine, then picture an average urban street, a row of North-Circular Tudor semis down each side with you standing in the middle of the road (do this early one Sunday morning). Then try to picture everything covered in a mound of shingle, with the pile rising steeply from the far end of the gardens on one side to completely cover both rows of houses and then gently sloping away beyond the end of the gardens on the other side, then think of that pile stretching for 18 miles. Impressive isn't it?

50°35.2'N 2°29.2'W

Fisherman's boathouse by The Fleet

There have been attempts at estimating the weight of all that material. Apparently 100 million tonnes is thought to be a reasonable figure.

If that isn't mind-boggling enough, consider this. The shingle is graded along Chesil's length, being pea size at the West Bay end and fist size at the Portland end. This phenomenon is linked to the fetch. The Bank faces south-west, the prevailing winds and 5,000 miles of open sea. It's not surprising then that the waves from that direction have more power than those from the south, which are only generated in the Channel. Consequently the former can carry the larger material all the way along the Bank to Portland, but the latter can only manage to move the smaller pieces in the opposite direction.

My visit to Chesil Bank was made in December 2001 during the week that the Dorset and East Devon coast was granted World Heritage Site status, placing it on a par with the Grand Canyon and the Great Barrier Reef. This is mainland Britain's first natural site to receive such recognition, the others – Avebury, Hadrian's Wall and Bath, for instance – are all man made. The recognition has been attained because of its outstanding geology, being an almost complete record of 180 million years of history centred on the Jurassic period.

Chesil Bank, however, does not fit into that time scale, being a newcomer to the area in the last 10,000 years. It is thought to be created out of the local rock debris deposited by meltwater at the end of the last ice-age, which was then pushed back by the rising sea levels to form a storm beach. The low-lying land behind it became flooded forming The Fleet, an eight miles long tidal lagoon connected to the sea through a narrow channel into Portland Harbour.

Both Chesil Bank and The Fleet are natural treasures in their own right, but together they make a rare and sensitive habitat, home to many scarce plants and birds.

To protect the plants and breeding or over-wintering birds, access to the section of the Bank adjoining The Fleet is severely restricted. There is no right of way along it, but from 1st September to 30th April access is allowed on the seaward side only. Between 1st May and 31st August it is closed altogether.

To see the Bank at its most impressive I would recommend a visit to the Portland end, where there is a large car park next to the visitor centre. Pay them a visit, they are very friendly and helpful with lots of leaflets, booklets, exhibits, information and good advice.

From the visitor centre Chesil has the appearance of a railway embankment. The landward side of the Bank is stable and the gradient even, but after crossing the broad ridge you will find that the seaward side has been shaped into a number of terraces or ridges that vary in width, height and firmness, the profile being constantly changed by the sea.

The day of my visit looked like being the last guaranteed sunny day of the year, with a stationary area of high pressure over the North Sea bringing frosty and foggy starts to days that were calm, cold and bright.

Reaching the ridge gave my first view of the almost flat, blue sea of Lyme Bay and as I stepped down across the terraces toward it came silence, with shelter from the noise of the traffic on the Weymouth to Portland road.

There was a very slight swell from the south, hardly anything at all, but the point at which the sea met the shingle was at first hidden from view by a last, small ridge and not even that interaction could be heard.

On reaching the water's edge I could see and hear a succession of small waves striking the shingle at an angle, each one creating a swirling semi-circular splash of foaming sea that danced rapidly along the steeply sloping shoreline, followed immediately by its dark antithesis the powerful backwash, noisily sucking the shingle away from the Bank before the next sparkling wave chased it away in the direction of West Bay.

I could have sat and watched this mesmerising display of Mother Nature's kinetic art all day. Is this work?

Almost every piece of rubbish that falls or is discarded into the sea in Lyme Bay or the western Channel seems eventually to come ashore on Chesil Bank. The ridge is scattered with odd pieces of wood, fragments of fishing net, innumerable plastic bottles and even, that day, a piece of timber the size of a telegraph pole with about two dozen truck tyres threaded onto it.

The Bank is a noted ships graveyard and bad weather even brings whales or dolphins ashore occasionally. In the eighteenth century the sea washed up what was rumoured to be a mermaid, but it turned out to be a dead camel.

Among the rubbish are pieces of well-rusted metal, possibly fragments of winches that were once used to draw fishing boats up the shingle, but some have been identified as pieces of the *Royal Adelaide*, an emigrant ship that was wrecked off here in 1872. The vessel was also carrying a cargo of schnapps and a number of looters apparently died of exposure after getting drunk and passing out.

In the very worst conditions imaginable the sea has been known to break over the Bank, even depositing ships in the lagoon. The damage caused on such occasions to the communities that live near the shore of the landward side of The Fleet is well described in the second chapter of John Meade Faulkner's novel *Moonfleet*, a romantic tale of adventure and smuggling set in the village of Fleet and centred around Moonfleet Manor, a real house that's now the *Moonfleet Hotel*.

In winter animal and plant life on the Bank is sparse, the occasional gull guards the shoreline and on the lower slopes of the landward side there's a patchy mat of sea campion. On this side you will find a collection of fishermen's boathouses, small, tarred, timber buildings. Some are surrounded with the paraphernalia of the trade, including the remains of a few traditional boats peculiar to Chesil; the lerret, a rowing boat that's pointed at the bow and stern and used for seine netting in Lyme Bay, and the trow, a flat bottomed boat used on the Fleet.

Not far from the visitor centre an area has been fenced off to provide a safe haven for little terns. Spending the autumn and winter in West Africa these are some of Britain's rarest sea birds. They return to Chesil Bank in April to breed (might one say 'one good tern deserves another'?), making their nests on the shingle, which provides good camouflage for their eggs. The area gives protection from clumsy humans and predatory foxes and enables them to be better monitored through the laying and rearing period.

If you want to see them, come in June or July when you can also enjoy the plant life of the shingle at its most colourful, but if you want to enjoy Chesil in peace and isolation like I did, then a bright December day is just perfect, but don't be like the looters of the *Adelaide*, wrap up warm and just get drunk on the wonder of it.

SOUTH BY WEST

BOLT HEAD
DEVON

You can be excused just this once if you are not familiar with the Salcombe area. It is that part of south Devon that projects into the English Channel between Plymouth and Torbay with Dartmoor to the north. It is a pleasantly isolated position.

I first became aware of it many years ago when my bank manager retired. I had one of those worrying "would you like to make an appointment to see me?" telephone calls, only to find to my relief that he was commissioning me to paint a picture of the place he was retiring to; Salcombe.

His successor also summoned me to his office for a similar conversation, this time he was spending a little more money; the bank's.

If I may digress a little further; it's funny where these things lead. Eventually my paintings (being at that time mostly on an agricultural theme) adorned the bank's stand at the Smithfield Show in London from which came a wonderful article, a double page spread in colour in *Farmers Weekly*. My local newsagent had never sold so many copies in one week.

This came at a time when I was becoming more settled in my work and it gave a great boost to my confidence.

Not long before that I had taken part with a friend in an exhibition that had been reviewed in an art magazine. This critique of our efforts was mildly approving without being over-enthusiastic and we had both felt that the reviewer had somehow missed the point, focusing more on the technical aspects of our work: 'When using pastel the colour becomes broader and is freed from detail, and there is a greater sense of the continuity that is inherent in the land' was the tone of the piece.

My artist friend was a regular buyer of *Farmers Weekly* (I suspect only because he lived in a rented farm cottage and wanted to impress his landlord) and was as delighted with the Smithfield article as I was. We both felt that, unlike the art reviewer, the agriculture journalist had understood the intent behind the paintings, had seen them as images of a subject she worked with and knew well, not focusing on the marks made on the paper but seeing through the surface of the picture to the view beyond.

It is moments like that which make this work so rewarding.

The paintings are only a means to an end. The intention is not to create a collection of lovely marks for the viewer to admire (in fact, I do my best to

disguise my brush strokes) but to encourage a response to the subject of the painting. In this instance it had worked.

Sixteen years and a change in my preferred subject matter separate my two paintings of this part of Devon and this time my subject was not down at sea level but 120 metres up on the cliffs at Bolt Head, a mile to the south of Salcombe.

You know how it is when something sets off an annoying tune that goes round in your head and you just cannot get rid of it. I don't know why, but I cannot hear or read the name Bolt Head without thinking of that 1950s black and white American television show *The Munsters*, about a weird family of horror movie stereotypes. I see a hearse-like hot-rod pull up outside a large sinister looking Gothic villa and the head of the household, Herman Munster clambers out. He is the Frankenstein's monster character, his heavy browed flat-top head is held on with a bolt through the neck. Bolt neck – Bolt Head; you can see my problem.

My vision is not altogether inappropriate. The rock formations on the cliffs around Bolt Head have a somewhat weird, even bizarre look to them, a great contrast to the gentleness of the neighbouring countryside. I could imagine that lit by moonlight, with an owl hooting in the distance, the strange shapes found there might create a spooky atmosphere.

If Delia Smith was Mother Nature (and some would no doubt argue that she is) she might explain how to create such a landscape using the following recipe.

Take a hillside of clayey sedimentary rock and mash gently and slowly for a period, Devonian at least. Place into a mountain-forming press, if it's large enough the one you use for pressing tongue will do. Set to medium - the grade past the one you would normally use for slate making and leave to metamorphose at room temperature for a couple of aeons. You will know it is ready when the minerals have aligned themselves with the force of pressure. Check by breaking off a small piece, you should see the characteristic banding with lots of shiny mica fragments glistening in the light. Remove from the press and, to finish off, leave outside to weather. It should break into rough crags and stand out in irregular rugged points. For complete satisfaction donate to the National Trust.

By various gifts and acquisitions by public subscription the Trust owns about six miles of the coast in the vicinity of Bolt Head and has done so since the 1930s. Starting in the west at the small village of Hope Cove a footpath climbs onto the cliffs at Bolt Tail where there is an Iron Age fort. From here it passes across four and a half miles of unspoilt rugged clifftop to Bolt Head, dipping close to sea level only at Soar Mill Cove at about the midway point (I think this area should be renamed Bolt Waist).

For those unable or unwilling to make such a lengthy walk there is a National Trust car park at Bolberry Down between the coves of Hope and Soar Mill.

All along the coast the views are spectacular. Out to sea to the west, visibility permitting, can be seen the famous Eddystone lighthouse standing on a distant outcrop of the same rock that distinguishes the cliff tops here. At the eastern end of the walk from the vantage points of Bolt Head and nearby Sharp Tor are wonderful views north-west to the distant high peaks of Dartmoor, north-east across the

50°12.5′N 3°47.6′W

Bolt Head across Starehole Bay

Salcombe Estuary and further east along the coast as far as Prawle Point.

A manageable three mile round trip to Bolt Head and back can be made from Overbecks, by National Trust standards a modest Edwardian house with a curious collection of artefacts and set in a glorious cliffside sub-tropical garden. If it is open try to plan your 'stroll' so that you can finish here. Give yourself plenty of time and wear stout shoes as there are many places where the hard, sharp rock is exposed.

If you find Mother Nature's Bolt Head cliffs recipe a little demanding and need some refreshment at Overbecks while you rest your weary limbs, Nicola

Barlow's scones with Devon clotted cream are to be highly recommended. They're made to a recipe of which I'm sure Delia would approve.

By then you will be glad of somewhere to rest and the delicious refreshments will seem even more satisfying.

I set off along the path from the small car park at Overbecks having forgotten my OS map, therefore not quite knowing what to expect, but remembering enough to be aware that I would be climbing to about 120 metres in quite a short distance.

Sure enough the path took me up the steep hillside behind the house, through a wood and eventually levelling out with open fields to my right and the gorse covered cliffs to my left. This is it I thought, a bit strenuous at first, but now the gentle wander out to Bolt Head to look forward to.

Imagine then my dismay when I reached Sharp Tor and looked down into Starehole Bay, a stunning view it has to be said, but then came the realisation that between me and my destination was a valley, Starehole Bottom. To cross the valley the path heads inland a short distance falling as it does almost to sea level, where the climb back up to 120 metres begins all over again. There is then, of course, the thought that this will have to be repeated on the return journey.

Painful as it may seem at the time, once you have recovered you will be in no doubt that it was worth the effort.

SOUTH-SOUTH-WEST

LOE BAR
CORNWALL

As soon as you cross the border from Devon into Cornwall you are made aware that you are entering a different realm. The county's flag, a white cross on a black background is a frequent sight, a sign of an independent spirit proclaiming that Cornwall is more than just the remotest county in England. It has its own history, culture and language and the Cornish are proud of the differences.

If a place name here is not prefixed with Saint, then it is more than likely to begin Tre... Lan... Pen... or Porth... indicating that the county's heritage is closely linked with that of Wales and Brittany. Even more obviously English sounding place names can leave one puzzled as to their origin. Here are a couple to contemplate: Indian Queens, a village between Bodmin and Truro, and London Apprentice, a hamlet to the south of St Austell.

On the journey along the A30 down the spine of the county can be seen evidence of Cornwall's unique industrial past. Scattered across an otherwise rural and sometimes wild looking landscape are occasional sightings of the spoil heaps from china clay workings and the distinctive remains of tin and copper mine engine houses, narrow tall buildings with even taller chimneys attached. Time is slowly blending these into the landscape. The few ugly sights today are a product of the county's tourist industry. Signs proclaiming 'bar meals served all day', 'home made clotted cream teas' and 'fresh baked Cornish pasties' assault us from all directions.

My initial port of call was a town which, because of what has happened at my ultimate destination, is no longer a port.

The River Cober flows to the west of Helston, entering the sea two and a half miles away to the south of the town. Once standing at the head of the Cober's estuary, Helston was in its day a small but important port, but there has not been a Cober Estuary since the thirteenth century. This is not a case of the river silting up, the former estuary is still full of water, but now it is Loe Pool or The Loe, Cornwall's largest natural freshwater lake.

The reason for this change can be found nearby on the coast between the little port of Porthleven and Gunwalloe Cove.

Loe Bar has something in common with Chesil Beach. A shingle bank, it has gradually grown across the mouth of the River Cober eventually damming it. The Bar is now about 500 metres long and 180 wide,

50°04.4'N 5°17.3'W

with the sea on one side and Loe Pool, about ten metres higher on the other.

Loe Bar's origin is a little unclear. It is thought that a combination of onshore and longshore drift brought along material which built up on both sides of the entrance to the river estuary. With the gradual accumulation of material the two spits grew together until they eventually joined forming one.

No doubt while a natural channel still existed, the two separate spits provided some protection for the boats sailing in and out of Helston. That may even be the reason why a port developed here. Eventually however the combined forces of man and the river were no longer able to keep the narrowing channel open. One theory is that the final damming was caused by a great storm which drove a massive amount of material ashore.

The source of the material which makes up Loe Bar is itself something of a puzzle. Almost ninety per cent of it is flint. If this has been removed and carried by the sea from somewhere else along the coast then it must have travelled all the way from east Devon where the nearest source is to be found, a journey of about 120 miles. It is, of course, possible that the source is hidden on the sea bed somewhere offshore and the material is brought in by the tide.

There are a number of ways to gain access to the Bar, which is owned by the National Trust. The Trust also owns Loe Pool and a considerable amount of land around it, the Penrose Estate, which was given to them in 1974 (making them only the third owners since Helston ceased to be a port). Not all of the land has public access, but there are a number of footpaths across it and a five mile walk round The Loe which includes most of the Bar.

I approached the Bar on foot from a car park on the low cliffs to the east of Porthleven, a walk of a little over half a mile round a couple of rocky headlands with low sandy cliffs between. The footpath meets the path round the west side of Loe Pool next to Bar Lodge, an attractive stone built Victorian villa.

Attached to the gate of Bar Lodge was a notice warning of the dangers lurking within the waters of The Loe. Streams flowing into it are rich in phosphates and nitrates and periodically a toxic blue/green algae forms, de-oxygenating the water and suffocating whatever lives within it.

One occupant of The Loe is believed by some to be the Lady of the Lake from the Arthurian legends. This is where Tennyson makes a reprise.

In his poem *Morte d'Arthur* he describes the location for the scene where a dying Arthur is taken after battle by Sir Bedivere to a resting place. Here Arthur instructs the knight to return his sword Excalibur, the source of his power and status, to the lake, which, understandably, Sir Bedivere is somewhat loath to do. Tennyson's description could be of Loe Bar.

> *…And bore him to a chapel nigh the field,*
> *A broken chancel with a broken cross,*
> *That stood on a dark strait of barren land.*
> *On one side lay the Ocean, and on one*
> *Lay a great water, and the moon was full.*

No doubt there are other locations which fit that description, Chesil Beach for instance, but there is, close by at Gunwalloe, a church at the top of the beach which could be the 'chapel nigh the field'.

It's a romantic notion, I know, and when the toxic algae blooms the Lady of the Lake wouldn't last long without breathing aparatus. However, the theory

where Loe meets the sea

fails on dates. King Arthur is supposed to have lived in the sixth century, when The Loe was still the tidal estuary of the River Cober. If Tennyson knew Loe Bar and was inspired to place events there we should forgive him for not being aware of its relatively recent appearance, I am sure we all think of most natural change as a slow process.

At heart I am probably more inclined to the *Monty Python and the Holy Grail* version of events: "...strange women lying in ponds distributing swords is no basis for a system of government."

Like me you may be wondering how the water level of Loe Pool is maintained. The River Cober and various streams are constantly filling it, so why has it not turned the Bar into a weir?

At the Bar's western end a concrete culvert through the shingle acts as an overflow pipe. From the base of the low cliff below Bar Lodge a flat rocky outcrop extends across the beach concealing the culvert's exit. The excess freshwater of the Loe empties out across the rocks and into the sea.

At the time of my visit an incoming tide was

bringing the occasional foaming wave just far enough up the beach to reach the farthest rock. In King Arthur's time this would have been the moment at which the sea would begin to refill the Cober Estuary, when the modest flow of the river would have yielded to the overwhelming force of the sea and boats might have been preparing for entry into, or departure from, Helston. Instead we have man's compromise with nature, a pipe under the beach preserving this moment of equilibrium forever. I took this as the subject for my painting as this particular spot at this precise moment symbolised for me the changing nature of Loe Bar and Loe Pool.

Now, if the origin of Indian Queens still troubles you I have discovered the following, although there is not a definitive explanation:

The nineteenth century village takes its name from a coaching inn, originally called the *Queen's Head* which was built in about 1775 near the junction of two (then new) turnpikes. By 1787 the name had been changed to *The Indian Queen*, which became plural in the nineteenth century.

One story to explain who the Indian Queen was claims that Pocahontas stayed there. However, as she died in 1617 it is somewhat unlikely, don't you think? This myth is perpetuated by the naming of a lane in a 1960s housing estate (when the building was demolished to make way for it) *Pocahontas Crescent.*

Another more likely story was told in an inscription, later plastered over, on the porch of the inn. This was of a Portuguese Princess who landed by packet boat at Falmouth and stayed one night at the inn on her way to London. Her swarthy appearance gave the impression that she was an Indian. This one gets my vote.

For a time the inn's sign apparently had the portrait of an Indian Queen on one side and Queen Victoria as Empress of India on the other.

What of London Apprentice? I will leave you to investigate that one and if you are game for a challenge here are a few more to grapple with; Bone, Bottoms, Bugle, Cripplesease, Flushing, Gummow's Shop, Herodsfoot, Playing Place, Retire, Sticker, Three Hammers, Twelveheads . . .

SOUTH-WEST BY SOUTH

WEST PICKARD BAY
PEMBROKESHIRE

Some English readers are going to find this hard to believe, but I once suffered sunstroke in Wales. At the time I had been living there for nearly three years and somehow felt obliged to make the best of the occasion when the sun finally appeared. Only joking; but the sunstroke was real enough.

On my journey along the M4 motorway to Pembrokeshire I passed the place where those formative years were spent, where I eventually 'found myself' as an artist. The urge to revisit the building where I took the most significant steps in my development proved too strong to resist and I made a short detour to find what I knew then as Newport College of Art.

Alas, the red brick Edwardian Baroque building that held so many fond memories was boarded up and derelict. The rest of the area was looking a bit sad, too. I remembered that Newport had its moments of delight, but on the whole kept them well hidden, so perhaps its newly acquired Golden Jubilee City status (announced within a week of my visit – no connection I'm sure) will herald a revival.

During my years there I received from some of my fellow students informal education in the correct pronunciation of Welsh place names, knowledge that has stayed with me and proved useful, if not always wholly convincing.

The key is to master the *Ll* sound that begins many names. Place the tongue firmly behind the upper front teeth and breathe out; never use *cl* or even *thl*. It is also important to know that *dd* is pronounced as a hard *th* (as in *the*), that *c* and *g* are always hard, *f* is pronounced as a *v* (unless it is *ff*, which is an *f*), *w* can be either a consonant or a vowel with long and short pronunciations as if it was *oo*, and *y* is a vowel that can be pronounced as an *e*, *i* or *u*.

You can practice this as you drive around Wales as many of the road signs are in both languages (Welsh first) making these necessary eyesores twice the size they would otherwise be. If you are a visitor it is easy pass a sign before you find the name of the place you are heading for. If only we could agree one name and spelling for each place, then these blots on the landscape would at least be smaller blots.

In most cases the English version is an anglicised corruption (no doubt originating as a mispronunciation) of the correct name. On the signs along the M4 motorway the English name comes first and it's often easy to see the link when reading familiar names such as Cardiff/Caerdydd. Sometimes there is only one

51°39.6'N 5°05.5'W

name, the same in both languages (hooray!), Merthyr Tydfil for instance, but occasionally there will be a place where the English and Welsh names seem to bear no relation whatsoever, as in Swansea/Abertawe.

The use of English and Welsh for place names is of particular interest where I was heading for, south Pembrokeshire, an area that is known in England, at least, as Little England beyond Wales. The area, particularly around Tenby, has long been popular with English holidaymakers and South Pembrokeshire place names are predominantly English, a result of colonisation by the Normans that was successfully resisted by the inhabitants of north Pembrokeshire, where the place names remained Welsh.

My destination was a short section of the Pembrokeshire Coast Path, a long distance footpath of more than one hundred and eighty miles, created after the Pembrokeshire coast was made into a National Park in 1952. National Park is the highest designation that can be given to a landscape and is only applied to those of special natural beauty. The Pembrokeshire Coast is the only linear, essentially maritime National Park and is an old and varied landscape which man has used and occasionally abused from earliest times.

I joined the coast footpath at the north-west end of the dunes where it climbs onto the cliffs that have been created by the erosion of a ridge of Old Red Sandstone, some of the oldest rocks in Britain. At an average of 50 metres in height the cliffs here are relatively modest, but unfortunately that doesn't equate with a gentle stroll along the footpath.

Natural arch, West Pickard Bay

Faults in the sandstone have been exploited by the sea, which has cut a series of bays into the ridge. The first of these is unexceptional and easily negotiated, the path diverting inland a little and making it necessary to step down almost to sea level. Further on the bays become more substantial and are not so easily managed. Frankly, if you suffer from even the mildest form of vertigo, or just have problems with looking down from high positions, I imagine that you could find the first mile of this walk terrifying.

Walking over the headlands between the bays is not the problem, neither is passing round each one at the lowest point, often crossing a small wooden bridge that carries the path over a stream. It is the climb into and out of the bays that can be difficult, as it often means being perilously close to the cliff edge, sometimes with little in the way of good footholds; not much fun in a high wind with a heavy rucksack on your back, I would think.

After about a mile of this there is a stile with a notice which reads something like 'you are now entering a challenging section of the coast path', it's enough to make those of a nervous disposition scream with panic.

Beyond this stile the true meaning of the notice became apparent. The path does not become more frightening, in fact from that point of view the worst has already been negotiated, it's just very hard work, with steeper and deeper bays to climb in and out of.

The effort is worth it, however.

After crossing a broad headland well away from the cliff edge, brushing through thickets of wind-swept gorse, the path reaches a natural cliff top mound enclosed by the remains of a man-made bank and ditch on the landward side, the site of an iron age promontory fort, one of fifty along the Pembrokeshire coast. The bank and ditch would have been more of a barrier than they are now, possibly reinforced with stone and topped with a wooden palisade that would have extended round the cliff edge for safety; a symbol of an organised society.

It was hard to imagine it now, but from the early to mid iron age (800 to 400 BC) and possibly into the Romano-British period (up to 400 AD) this exposed site would have been a thriving community living in thatched timber roundhouses, a working village almost, where people might have grazed animals and cultivated crops such as wheat, beans and woad, fished from coracles and traded, probably with Ireland, possibly with the Phoenicians, when some of the major commodities would have been salt and people. Now there was just me, the rabbits and the ravens.

I was here during the first days of March, there was a cold westerly wind blowing and rain (which, thankfully, held off until I reached shelter) always looked imminent. In these conditions this seemed to be a particularly inhospitable location to settle, although the climate was likely to have been better then, but somehow I could not imagine the wind not blowing strongly across this exposed headland.

There was one aspect of this location, however, that provided more than adequate compensation for the conditions and made the walk worth doing; the amazing view that lay beyond it.

I had reached the east side of West Pickard Bay, the most substantial inlet along this section of the coast path, and in the grey gloom more akin to dusk than late morning I peered down from the top of a gully, as near to the cliff edge as I dare go for fear of being blown off into the abyss below. This was a wild and raw landscape; a dramatic meeting of land and sea, with rocks jagged and hard edged, blood red and black, with distinct layers of inclined and folded strata clearly exposed on the far side of the bay.

I tried to imagine being over on the other side looking back at myself standing on the edge. Beneath my feet all those layers of rock laid down over an unimaginable period of time on the bed of an ancient sea, pushed up, folded and crumpled by incredible power and then battered to its present appearance by churning seas; all that energy and all that history.

What have these cliffs seen, who and what has walked and swum and flown around here in all those millions of years? And now I am going to walk back along the path and climb into my little motorised metal and glass box, which is then going to take me away from here. What a strange and extraordinary world we live in.

SOUTH-WEST

PORTH NEIGWL

GWYNEDD

Hold out your lower right arm at 45°, bring your fingers together and stick out your thumb so it is pointing down, then imagine that this is the Llŷn Peninsula (which makes your head Anglesey and sitting on your left shoulder is a parrot called Llandudno). Porth Neigwl is a four miles long, south-west facing beach between your thumb and index finger.

The origin of the name Porth Neigwl is not known for certain. It could be Gaelic, or it could be derived from Nigel de Loreyng, who was granted extensive lands and estates in the area by Edward the Black Prince after his achievements during the Battle of Poitiers, a decisive engagement in the first phase of the Hundred Years War between England and France.

However, this is all academic because somehow the English name for it seems far more meaningful and appropriate, especially on the windy winter's day that I first encountered it; Hell's Mouth.

There is one theory that even this name might not be all it seems. Hell in this instance could be the Norse word for clear; as in Hell Gill in the Lake District or the railway station named Hell, 33 minutes north of Trondheim ('a super-saver return to Hell please'); and you thought it was only London commuter trains that took you to hell and back.

One local resident I spoke to informed me that it is also known as 'the vacuum cleaner of the peninsula', as the winds and tides seem to contrive to keep all the flotsam and jetsam from landing on the other beaches in the area and dump it all at Porth Neigwl. This was not just the odd plastic bottle, piece of timber or remnant of fishing net, but great mounds of rubbish, which I had to clamber over to get onto the beach; tree trunks, bags of peat, five gallon drums and plastic washing baskets in a better range of colours than Woolworths can muster.

During my two visits there were always a few visitors making their way along the beach with heads down, kicking through these piles of material for ... who knows what? Firewood perhaps, or some curiously shaped sea-rounded driftwood to make into sculpture, something useful for the garden or bathroom, an odd pair of Marigold gloves maybe – pink for left, orange for right. It's all there waiting to be discovered. No vacuum cleaners though; as far as my house is concerned James Dyson is already washed up.

When conditions are favourable, however, some of the visitors will only be looking to take home the memory of a great day spent on a surfboard, shooting tubes and hanging ten, as they say. If Porth

52°48.9'N 4°32.7'W

Surf's up

The village has a splendid and very informative web site – www.abersoch.co.uk – where potential surfers can get up-to-the-minute surf reports. One of the surf equipment shops sponsors a webcam, where you can view pictures of the beach that are updated every hour, just click on webcams and then Porth Neigwl and you are there.

I was pleased to discover there, too, a notice from the Porth Neigwl Coastcare Group who organise working parties to clear the rubbish off the beach and I contacted them to find out more. Understandably, as the beach gets comparatively few winter visitors they were not planning to start clearing until Easter, so the rubbish I encountered had been accumulating for nearly five months, since their last visit in October. It's a real community effort involving the Coastguards, young offenders on community service as well as local residents, and in the summer holiday-makers join in too. Only non-organic material is removed, which must help somewhat with the workload.

I reached Porth Neigwl from a small car park off a lay-by outside the tiny village of Llanengan, along a footpath of soft sand between fields of natural grassland where there are areas of gorse and the occasional pond. It opens out onto the beach through a break in the low cliffs that back it along its entire length.

The RNLI notice board in Abersoch indicated that a south-westerly gale had been recorded three hours

Neigwl is noted for anything it's for being a good surf beach.

The reason the surfing is so good here is that the beach looks through a 'surf window'. It is stuck out in the Irish Sea looking straight through the gap between St David's Head in Pembrokeshire and Carnsore Point in County Wexford, allowing it to pick up the Atlantic swells that squeeze through St George's Channel when the wind is blowing, as it so often does, from the south-west.

In nearby Abersoch, an attractive village of mostly Victorian and Edwardian houses with a small harbour and wonderful sandy beaches, the number of businesses that cater for surfers testifies to how big the sport has become here and how important it is for the local economy. When the surfing is good the accents you are most likely to hear are those from Manchester, Cheshire and the Wirral.

earlier and it was still blowing strong. The roar of the sea could be heard back at the car park. The tide was on its way out leaving about 30 metres of the gently shelving beach exposed. At the water's edge a layer of white foam carpeted the beach like a fall of snow, in sharp contrast to the dark grey pebbles that lay in bands over the coarse sand.

Low cloud enveloped the top of the 300 metre high hill Mynydd Rhiw (an unusual name as *mynydd* means mountain and *rhiw* hill) on the headland four miles away to the north-west. The light was poor and the air full of spray. You might say I was in the teeth of a gale in Hell's mouth. It was a brutal atmosphere, but nevertheless invigorating.

These seemed to be just the right conditions to show how the wind blows the lighter grains of sand off a beach to form the dunes that build up behind it. These dunes, however, had formed on top of the low cliff of boulder clay that is being cut back by the sea at a rate of 30 centimetres a year, so while the wind is slowly building the dunes up, the sea is removing them, leaving the material on the beach for the wind to blow it back… and so on.

When the tide is at its lowest the petrified stumps of a 5,000 year old forest are revealed in the bay, indicating just how far the cliff has receded in, geologically speaking, a short period of time.

I later discovered that I had seen the beach in an unusually sandless state. The dark pebbles that covered large areas of it are usually hidden beneath a layer of light-coloured sand, which had been removed by the rough seas that pounded the beach through the winter.

The next day dawned calm and sunny and I was eager to get onto the beach again to view it in more favourable conditions. Along the sandy footpath the sound of the sea had been replaced by the liquid call of the skylark and a pair of stonechats accompanied me along the way. I also came across a group of people speaking to each other in Welsh, and it then struck me as odd that this was my fourth day in the Principality and yet it was the first time I had heard people speaking their native tongue. With more than seventy five percent of those in the area using it as their first language this should have been the one place I was more likely to hear it.

On the beach I caught up with a couple of men carrying angling gear. They were going to spend the day casting for sea bass; this is a good place for it apparently, so good in fact they had driven all the way from Cheshire for this, stopping on the way to dig for bait and still managing to be here by 10 am.

This time the tide was further out and the beach appeared twice the size it had the previous day. Instead of grey silhouettes, the two headlands stood out crisp and clear in their natural colours, making them seem much closer and the beach feel more framed and enclosed. Also visible for the first time was Bardsey Island (or Ynys Enlli) a National Nature Reserve that sits two miles off the Mynydd Rhiw headland. In mediaeval times the Augustinian Abbey there was a place of pilgrimage, three trips there being considered the equivalent of one to Rome.

In the sunlight the gaudy unnatural colours of the plastic debris drew attention to itself even more so; somehow it had accumulated in coordinating piles, with one predominantly blue, one yellow and another orange.

The sea was calmer and quiet, the fury had subsided and been replaced with good beach walking weather, but I felt an overwhelming sense of disappointment and soon left. Where was the drama?

SOUTH-WEST BY WEST

RHOSNEIGR
ISLE OF ANGLESEY

At first I found it difficult to think of Anglesey as being an offshore island. The Menai Strait, that slice of sea separating it from the rest of Wales, looks no wider than some river estuaries and after the brief drive over Britannia Bridge I felt deprived of that sense of the crossing being an event. Once on the other side, though, the landscape changed considerably and it was clear I had arrived somewhere detached. In England you might call it gently undulating, but compared with the rest of Wales it would be fair to call it almost flat.

Visitors to the island are greeted by the Marquess of Anglesey; he doesn't shake you by the hand personally, but looks down from his 28 metres high column of Anglesey marble just off the A55. This of course is not the present Marquess, it's a bronze statue of the first one who, as William Henry Paget, Earl of Uxbridge, was second in command to Wellington and in charge of the cavalry at the Battle of Waterloo. It was there he had his right leg shattered by a French cannonball. At the time he and Wellington were side by side on horseback and the following conversation is alleged to have taken place.

Marquess; "Begod, there goes me leg."

Wellington; "Begod, so it do."

A replacement leg was fitted and it is now on display nearby at the family home Plas Newydd. The real leg is buried in a tomb at Waterloo.

The figure on the column is bipedal, presumably vanity and the skills of the leg-fitter's art combining to work such a wonder. This Marquess continues to serve his country and raises about £100,000 a year by allowing people to abseil down his column for charity.

To continue in the military vein, there are going to be quite a few people around Britain who know Rhosneigr well, but probably only from the air. Anyone since 1958 who has trained to fly front line fast jets for the RAF or the Royal Navy will have flown over Rhosneigr countless times on training flights, as it sits just short and a bit to port of the main runway at RAF Valley (or Fali as it alternatively appears on the road signs).

This is where the pilots come to learn their advanced flying and do their tactics and weapons training. About 60 trainees a year pass through Valley, each one spending a total of 100 hours in the air. It's all a little scary. Having them zooming around the skies all day in their shiny black Hawks is fine. Coming over at TV aerial level is no problem, even when you know they're wearing 'L' plates and you

53°12.6'N 4°29.8'W

can tell the colour of their eyes. It's when you encounter them in the pub in the evening that it hits you. They're barely old enough to be shaving!

It has to be said, Hawks are not the quietest aircraft in the world and on weekdays the roar of their engines is an almost constant presence, but you get used to it and it soon ceases to be a nuisance. Houses in Rhosneigr have their double glazing set with the two layers of glass several centimetres apart for soundproofing rather than thermal insulation (which would be a pointless exercise here judging by the number of palm trees you see around the village).

This soundproofing was paid for by the Ministry of Defence, but I understand it does not cover the village quite as comprehensively as the noise of the aircraft. One resident I spoke to told me that there is a road where the houses on one side have it and those on the other side don't. I asked at the base why this was so and was informed that who qualified was determined by how far they lived from the flight-path. "You've got to draw the line somewhere." Just like the sound does, no doubt.

It's not just the palm trees that indicate how mild the climate is here. On a wander around the village I noticed a number of hebes in full bloom and this was only early March, in most parts of the country they wouldn't be out until mid May. On the down side, during my short stay it always seemed to be windy, even when the weather forecast was suggesting it would be calm. Rhosneigr, twinned with Chicago.

The village's appearance is atypical of the area and has more the look of a suburb or a small town than a village. With many of the buildings being painted white there is something of an Isle of Wight, or at least south coast of England atmosphere, although some of the more plain, single storey buildings are as indicative of a Celtic community as any I have seen in the Hebrides or Ireland.

Rhosneigr was a fashionable resort in the Edwardian period. Today it may not have what everyone is looking for in a holiday destination, but still appeals to those who want somewhere out of the way to enjoy the simple pleasures of sun, sea and sand, if not Mediterranean temperatures. Surfing and wind-surfing are popular and scuba divers are attracted by the many wrecks in the area, notably the *Norman Court*, sister ship to the *Cutty Sark*, which lies in shallow water in the bay to the north of the village.

Like everywhere in offshore Britain from Shetland to the Scilly Isles, life here is pleasantly laid-back, there is very little traffic about apart from in the air and it seems to be, all things considered, a pleasant place to live, particularly if you are hard of hearing.

The village sits across a low ridge of rock which projects into the Irish Sea, with long, broad sandy beaches sweeping away to the north-west and the south-east, with nowhere except for RAF Valley of any consequence for several miles in either direction. The beach to the south-east, known locally as Broad Beach, Traeth Llydan on Ordnance Survey maps, was the location I had come here to paint.

Arriving late in the afternoon on a rather dull and breezy day, I spent the hour or so before dusk just walking along the beach contemplating my subject and hoping that a brighter day would follow.

The rounded shape of Holyhead Mountain, at a modest 220 metres the highest point on Anglesey, was all that could be seen to the north-west beyond Rhosneigr; it is nine miles away but looks much closer. To the south the beach ends at a low grass covered headland topped by Barclodiad Y Gawres, a

5,000 year-old burial chamber that is one of the most important neolithic sites in Wales.

The entrance to the earth-covered chamber faces north along the beach and forms one branch of a cross. In the other chambers were found the cremated remains of several humans as well as those of a frog, a mouse, a shrew, a hare, a whiting, a snake, a pig and a number of eels, but the most interesting aspect of the chamber is the delicate carvings to be found on six of the massive stones with which it was constructed. Spirals, squares, rectangles, chevrons, arrows and grooves can all be seen in remarkable condition. Bring a torch as it's dark inside. The place is protected by a padlocked iron grill, so you need to collect a key from the Wayside Shop in Llanfaelog.

The place's name translates into English as The Giantess's Apronful; the legend being that the stones the giantess had been carrying to build a fortification were dropped here when the strings of her apron broke. Another legend tells of a cave a mile underground below the chamber, where King Arthur hid his royal treasury, still awaiting discovery. The cave's entrance is said to be revealed at exceptionally low tides.

Across the beach and offshore there are areas of rock, two of which are almost as substantial as headlands, effectively dividing the beach into three. Others are lower and when exposed by the falling tide reveal rock pools sitting between jagged peaks like a mountain range in miniature.

Rock pools in such a striking setting were something I had not so far encountered on these travels and I returned the next morning in bright sunlight to look for a suitable view with a comfortable dry seat from which to work. Had it not been for the blue sky reflected in the pools and the vivid green of the sea cabbage that adorned some of the rocks, the other-wise monochromatic scene would have worked well simply as a detailed pencil study. It was one of those occasions where I knew instantly that this was going to be a great subject.

looking along Traeth Llydan to Rhosneigr

WEST-SOUTH-WEST

CLEVELEYS

LANCASHIRE

My 1949 edition of *Lovely Britain* does not mention Cleveleys.

I first came here in February 1978 and remember it as cold, wet and windy with hardly any sight of the sun. This time it is the second week in June 2000 but the weather seems to have forgotten to turn over the intervening pages of its diary. The rain, in fact, was falling so hard that it seemed pointless stepping out of the car to retrieve my brolly from the boot. This brief encounter with the outside world beyond my climate-controlled haven would have been like taking a cold shower in the downdraught from a helicopter.

I thought of going into the Citizens Advice Bureau to ask if they knew what I was doing here.

I drove around the town for a while to get my bearings and to see what I could recognise from my previous visit and if I could find the hotel I had stayed in all those years ago. An improvement in the weather looked unlikely so eventually I gave up and decided that my time could be more productively spent driving to another compass point, hoping that the rain might have eased a little by the time I arrived there.

Being so close to my original starting point in the Forest of Bowland (it's only 22 miles away as the oystercatcher flies) meant that there was a cluster of points nearby. I needed to be aiming for somewhere further afield. The two in the area around Barrow in Furness looked like the ones to go for, being about 75 miles away, so I set off for them with the intention of returning a few days later when conditions might be ever so slightly better. For the next two hours I sampled the delights of the northbound M6 motorway, where a 50 mph dash through the spray from the heavy trucks provided slightly improved visibility.

While I am away, here is some information about the area to keep you entertained. After all, entertainment is what this part of the Lancashire coast is all about.

Cleveleys is sandwiched between Fleetwood to the north and Blackpool to the south, although those two places would no doubt claim that they are the meat and Cleveleys is the packing that provides the roughage.

Around the world there are a number of towns and cities that have been 'twinned' with a neighbour

53°53.0'N 3°03.0'W

and become for ever linked by name like Buda and Pest or Minneapolis and St Paul and here in Lancashire we have another pairing. Cleveleys is rarely mentioned without its name being preceded by that of its conjoined inland neighbour Thornton.

From the casual visitors' point of view it is quite difficult to know where one of these Fylde towns ends and the next begins, particularly along the sea front where a road runs for several miles, overlooked by hotels and blocks of flats on the landward side and the famous trams on the other.

Heading south, although the change from Cleveleys is gradual, by the time you reach downtown Blackpool the transformation is of Dr Jekyll and Mr Hyde proportions. I have heard that Bill Bryson once likened visiting Blackpool to wading through the contents of someone else's stomach. I definitely got the impression that if you were brave enough to hang around until the pubs and take-aways closed you would find much of the night's consumption splattered across the pavement. Mingling with the crowds I felt strangely elderly (I haven't hit 50 yet), surrounded by gangs of young lads in this month's Man. United away shirts and 16 year old tarts wearing little more than a smile and a shower of the latest designer scent.

promenade shelter

Suddenly I had the urge to look up kitsch in the dictionary.

To the north is Fleetwood which gives the impression that its past has been more glorious than its present. It used to be the northern terminus of the railway line from London Euston, with connections by sea to Ireland and Scotland, and also a major deep-sea trawler port, the west coast's equivalent of Hull. Its men-folk were no doubt as familiar with the cold and treacherous waters off Iceland and the Arctic as they were with the elegant Victorian villas that overlook the tram lines still linking it to Cleveleys and Blackpool.

Now it is pleasantly subdued. One day it might be slightly grand again. I hope so.

Cleveleys sea-front on a blustery – but at least bright – Sunday morning is a good place to be if you want to avoid the crowds. Unlike at Blackpool, here I felt strangely young. The elderly dawdled along the smooth, flat, pink tarmac of the promenade and occasionally stopped for a rest at one of its many hipped-roofed shelters and stared out to sea where a solitary wind-surfer had braved the chill to take advantage of the reliable breeze. I sat and did the staring-out bit as well. Oh, to have the time to do this when you are young enough to need it!

Is it only in England that those of more mature years always seem to be clutching a slim, square, maroon nylon shopping bag with prominent white saddle stitching and a ten centimetres too long zip across the top?

Unlike them, though, my thoughts were not 'I can remember pushing the twins along here in their pram in 1951' but 'Now that I'm here, what am I going to find to paint?'

I wandered down to the beach and contemplated the possibilities there. Lots of groynes again, but the're not half as impressive as the ones at Goring. You really can't fight Mother Nature can you? She always gets her own way in the end.

A frothy, silty brown sea sprayed over the groynes. I looked back at the promenade, noticing a small ice cream caravan in the traditional egg-yellow and off-white livery being unhitched from a Mondeo. Where did those colours come from and why haven't they changed along with ice cream making technology? Where are the vans with the lime green and cherry ripple paint jobs? You can do wonders with computers and transfers these days.

I was obviously in one of those 'life, the universe and everything' moods.

Behind the caravan a line of brightly coloured green and blue beach huts caught my eye. I should correctly refer to them as beach bungalows – available for daily hire, each one equipped with cooking facilities and a table and chairs (for more information try www.cleveleys.co.uk). Realising that up there was where I needed to be, not down here with the flotsam and dog walkers, I returned to the stability of the pink tarmac. In my absence children had appeared. It's always the old folk that are out first isn't it? Preparing minors for the great outdoors is always a time consuming affair – rousing and dressing, then feeding, hosing down and re-dressing, with an allowance for tantrum time. Before they were old enough to go to university it took even longer.

The beach bungalows I supposed could be almost anywhere, they did not exactly shout Cleveleys at me, but that ice cream caravan … there was a certain ironic optimism about it. Now that was very Cleveleys.

WEST BY SOUTH

PILLING MARSH
LANCASHIRE

Driving away from Cleveleys across the flat Fylde farmland I was acutely aware of heading for a landscape which I had not before considered as a subject for painting.

When I started working in watercolour it seemed only natural to look for inspiration in the Wiltshire landscape I had adopted as home. There was a need to express my thoughts, feelings and fascination for not only its great natural beauty, but also the history of the land, which had been worked by man for so long that some of the surviving structures from the earliest communities there are as old as the pyramids.

My interest was primarily in the land. The paintings were often views across rolling downland, looking across, up to, or down from gently rounded hills, usually in sunlight. There was a solid, sculptural three-dimensional quality about the landscape which I enjoyed working with, it always looked so enticing. Often the paintings were nearly all land with a little strip of sky across the top.

Over time my reverence for the work of Mother Nature came more to the fore, particularly where I found elemental power most awe-inspiring, on the coast. I became captivated by the interaction of land and sea and man's often pathetic attempts to fight it.

The lack of sunlight which I sometimes encountered did not seem to matter that much any more, even the weather itself became the subject of some of the work. My horizons had changed.

Now I was driving to somewhere which I knew was going to be flat and open and I felt a little apprehensive. How would I tackle it?

It's not that it was a totally unfamiliar environment. As a child I had spent most summer holidays in the flat open countryside along the north Norfolk coast. The contrast between this and the thickly wooded undulations of Northamptonshire I grew up with, where distant views were almost non existent, could hardly be greater. That quiet corner of Norfolk was a place where the tide ebbed and flowed at walking pace across a vast expanse of firm rippling sands, where roads down to the shore across low reeded marshland were covered by the sea at high tide, where Canada geese seemed to outnumber humans and the skies were big.

I was hoping that Pilling Marsh would not be too much of a shock.

When I arrived at the car park/picnic area at the end of a short lane off the coast road between Cleveleys and Lancaster, only one other vehicle was

53°56.5'N 2°53.3'W

present. In front of me an embankment obscured my view of … what? I wondered.

On the way in I had passed an information board and before climbing the embankment to see what awaited me on the other side I walked back to read it:

Please do not disturb the birds
Wyre-Lune Sanctuary is a National Wildfowl Refuge, which was created in 1963 by the joint efforts of Morecambe Bay Wildfowlers Association and Fylde Wildfowlers Association in conjunction with the Duchy of Lancaster, other landowners and English Nature.

I was intrigued by the reference to wildfowlers which seemed to be out of place in a wildfowl refuge, this was something I needed to investigate.

Back to the embankment and whatever lay beyond. The sky had recently clouded over, but the western horizon was still bright. At six o'clock on a June evening there should be plenty of daylight left, but the temperature had dropped noticeably in the last hour and I did not expect the light to improve.

The embankment is a grass-covered sea wall that extends for about nine miles along the coast, protecting the low-lying farmland behind.

Standing on it, I looked out. It was obviously low tide, in fact the sea was barely visible, only as a silvery grey strip near the horizon to the north-west. At least six miles away to the north stood the rectangular mass of the Heysham nuclear power station and behind that, hardly visible at all, I could just make out the faintest blue silhouette of the southern hills of the Lake District. To my left the embankment curved away gradually, round the west side of Pilling Marsh. The land was so flat that the one feature of this view which stood out clearly was a small wood about two miles away, which just about

anywhere else would have gone almost unnoticed. To my right the embankment swept away to the east, with the northernmost hills of the Forest of Bowland as a backdrop.

In my immediate vicinity the grassy embankment fell away to what I assumed to be, at high tide, the shoreline. Beyond that for a few metres was an area of flat grassland with the occasional elongated pool of water marking its edge and then, stretching out for several hundred metres, the saltmarsh. In the distance all there seemed to be between the seaward edge of the marsh and the nuclear power station were the flat sands of the River Lune's estuary.

The saltmarsh was an extraordinary sight. It is a vast expanse of grassland, shimmering with colour which seems to be at the same time a mid to dark brown, a dusky pink and several shades of green, the all over evenness broken only by innumerable creeks and interconnecting channels, some containing water, which cut through the flatness of the marsh. A few patches of firmer grassland extended out into the marsh from the embankment.

I wanted to go out onto it, to take a closer look, but aware of its importance as a protected habitat I thought it wise to remain on the embankment

I was not alone. The saltmarsh's only occupant was a solitary shelduck, but the embankment and the firmer looking areas of the marsh were populated by a flock of about one hundred sheep and lambs, mostly in small family groups, some sitting down, some grazing and others just standing around, no doubt wary of my presence. I began to make my way slowly along the embankment trying not to disturb them. This was one aspect of the situation I was familiar with. The chalk downland in which I used to paint was often dotted with grazing sheep and

watch with mother

occasionally one or two would be allowed to wander into a painting. I had decided that, assuming I did not frighten them, I would try to manoeuvre myself into a position where I could include some in this painting. Having found a suitable spot I knelt down for a while so they could get used to my presence before I started working.

As I returned to the car I wondered how I could find out more about the saltmarsh habitat and why it is so important for wildfowl.

Eventually I tracked down English Nature's man with special responsibility for the site, who was able to provide me with some answers.

The River Lune Estuary is a Site of Special

Scientific Interest covering almost seven thousand hectares. The Sanctuary protects the intertidal roosts of important numbers of wildfowl and wading birds such as pink-footed goose, oystercatcher, grey plover, knot, turnstone, curlew, bar-tailed godwit, redshank, dunlin, shelduck, mallard and wigeon. The intertidal flats, exposed for long periods at low tide, are rich in invertebrates which some, shelduck for instance, depend on almost entirely for their diet. The site is a major link in the chain of estuaries down the west coast of Britain, a staging-post used by birds migrating between their breeding grounds in the far north and their wintering grounds a little further south, a sort of Travelodge and Welcome Break rolled into one.

Pink-footed geese for instance will fly down from Iceland in late September and October and stay for a while on the Ribble Estuary or the Wildfowl and Wetlands Trust's refuge at Martin Mere near Southport, both to the south. In late December and early January they will move north to the southern part of the Lune Estuary where they stay until mid to late March feeding on the surrounding pastures. From here they will move on to south-west Scotland for another feed before returning non-stop to Iceland.

The significance of a site is determined by the numbers of each species it regularly supports. For some birds it might be of national importance and for others it could be of international importance. For instance, to be of international importance for wintering waders it must have a total count of 20,000 birds, a figure which this one exceeds comfortably with an annual winter average of 26,500.

The marsh is also rich in plant life, particularly grasses and other salt-tolerant species. The sheep and sometimes cattle that have traditionally grazed the marsh create a fine sward which the wildfowl and waders like.

So, how do you count 26,500 waders?

There is no fool-proof scientific way of doing this, it's a guesstimate. First you have to count 100 birds quickly. With a picture in your mind of how much space they take up, you then divide that into the space they all take up and work out your total from that. You have to be able to do this quickly as they could be in flight at the time.

Where did the wildfowlers come in? Well, they don't. Their part in all this is that they keep away and let the birds have the place to themselves.

WEST TO NORTH

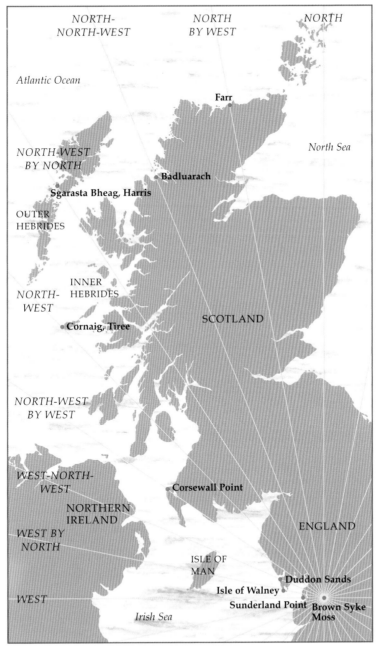

NORTH-
NORTH-WEST

NORTH
BY WEST

NORTH

Atlantic Ocean

Farr

North Sea

NORTH-WEST
BY NORTH

Badluarach

Sgarasta Bheag, Harris

OUTER
HEBRIDES

INNER
HEBRIDES

NORTH-
WEST

SCOTLAND

Cornaig, Tiree

NORTH-WEST
BY WEST

WEST-NORTH-
WEST

Corsewall Point

NORTHERN
IRELAND

ENGLAND

WEST BY
NORTH

ISLE OF
MAN

Duddon Sands

Isle of Walney

WEST

Sunderland Point

Brown Syke
Moss

Irish Sea

WEST

SUNDERLAND POINT

LANCASHIRE

For about the last seven miles of its course before it enters the sea the River Lune flows roughly parallel with the coast, creating a small peninsula about three miles wide. The last bridging point over the Lune is in the centre of the city of Lancaster, which during the twentieth century has expanded to join with its neighbour, the resort of Morcambe forming a continuous built-up area across the north of the peninsula.

To the south of this urban environment, between the Lune and Morecambe Bay is a pleasant, peaceful patch of farmland inhabited by three small villages and a hamlet. My destination was the tiny hamlet, Sunderland Point, on the finger of land at the peninsula's southern tip.

As the pink-footed goose flies it is less than four miles from Pilling Marsh, but by road it's 15. Getting there can be something of an adventure in itself. The last half mile or so is not always that straight forward and it is wise to check a tide timetable before you attempt it. There cannot be many settlements on 'mainland' Britain where you need to do that.

Here was my chance to see extensive saltmarsh at close quarters, so close in fact that I had to drive through it. The road from the village of Overton to Sunderland Point is laid across Sunderland Marsh and as the narrow strip of tarmac carries you onto the marsh a large red sign attached to two metal posts warns: *Danger. Do not proceed when these posts are in water.*

On the other side of the marsh the road rejoins land and terminates at a small public parking area on a sloping gravel bank next to a high stone wall. As I removed my seat belt I glanced around and noticed a line drawn at eye level on the wall in front of one of the other cars. Above the line is written HIGH WATER MARK. I had a feeling that this could be my most eventful visit yet.

From here the road continues as a private track in front of a row of houses which faces east across the River Lune. A small collection of boats was hauled up alongside the track. The opposite bank of the river looked to be about a quarter of a mile away at its nearest point and, judging by the large expanse of silt that was exposed on either side and the small amount of water in the deep channel, it looked like the tide was at or near its lowest ebb.

I assumed it was safe to stay for a few hours but thought it best to enquire about the tides before I wandered too far.

53°59.8'N 2°53.0'W

WEST

Second Terrace view

The small group of houses are a collection of traditional two storey buildings. Although each house is clearly an individual building architecturally, most are joined together forming a terrace.

The end house is larger and grander than the others with an angular bay next to the corner. In front of this house on the opposite side of the track a line of large slabs at the river's edge creates the impression of a small quayside. At the end of the slabs stands a tall stone gate post topped with a carved stone ball.

The post and the bay of the end house frames a view further along the shore where, about 150 metres away, stands a second row of mostly three storey houses.

I can safely say I had not seen anything quite like this before.

Turning the corner by the bay window I found myself looking along a lane overhung with trees. The houses would make a great subject for painting, but I am supposed to be painting at the last landfall, which according to my map is the west facing shore at the end of this lane.

On the right behind the corner house stands a small stone cottage. A short elderly man in a red shetland sweater and a check cloth cap was tending his garden. He looked like he belonged here so I asked him if he knew how high the tide would come up and how long I had before the road was covered.

He called up to an open door situated on the first floor at the top of a flight of stone steps.

"Just over eight metres," came the reply.

"You'll be alright, that's not enough to cover the road" he added. "Only some of the spring tides cover the road. Eight out of every ten days we are OK, on the other two we are cut off in the middle of the day for three to four hours."

He explained that he once lived round the corner "on the front" and there the houses have guides built in front of the lower part of the door frame. A wooden panel is slid into the guide sealing off the front door to prevent flooding on the rare occasions when an unfortunate combination of wind and tide brings water over the quayside. He took me round to point them out.

After explaining the reason for my visit I began to ask more questions.

"There's a book about the place you know, it tells you the history, you might find it useful."

We went back to his cottage and a copy was produced. Just what I needed.

"You can buy it from the house at the end of the lane, it's my brother-in-law's."

We continued chatting for a while as I admired his collection of watercolours of the area and his impressive library of Wisden cricketers' almanacs, obviously he was a man with a mind for detail. Eventually I asked him about the author of the book and he revealed himself to be the writer, previously too modest to volunteer the information.

After thanking him for his help I made my way along the lane to the west shore, stopping on the way to buy a copy of *The Story of Sunderland Point*. It was a pleasant stroll of about a quarter of a mile under a glorious blue sky. The lane was lined with blackberry bushes, cattle lazed and grazed in fields framed by stone walls and the only sound was the song of a skylark; bliss. This to me was England at its best, if only we could bottle it and deliver it to every urban doorstep.

At the end of the lane I found myself standing on

the edge of Middleton Marsh, another area of saltmarsh which stretched before me for about half a mile. In the distance I could just make out the sandbank which lay beyond the marsh and went by the wonderful name of The Shoulder of Lune.

The high-water line was indicated by the usual odd assortment of flotsam (does someone actually sail round Britain throwing short pieces of coloured rope overboard?) and the scattered remains of a tree. Close by, the marsh mainly consisted of large areas of tussocky long grass interspersed with patches of firm turf. Within the areas of firmer ground lay pools of brackish water. Beyond this the marsh was inter-sected by numerous small channels and gullies, some were still filled with water but most exposed areas of silt which glistened dazzlingly in the bright sunlight.

This seemed to be a good opportunity to produce a painting that would complement the view of Pilling Marsh. Instead of standing back and painting the wider view as I had done there, I could go in close and pick out a small area to show the marsh in detail. I made my way across the marsh in search of a suitable area, treading carefully in case the ground was not as firm as it looked, jumping across the occasional gulley. An accident of some kind seemed almost inevitable, but somehow I managed to stay dry.

Usually when I feel satisfied that I have gathered all the material I need I am happy to leave and move on to another location, but on this occasion I wanted to linger and just enjoy being there. For once I wanted to come out of work mode, relax and just soak up the atmosphere, give myself a couple of hours holiday. I had discovered somewhere really special and needed to savour every moment there. If only there was a hotel or guest house.

Opening the latest addition to my reference library I sat down and leafed through the pages. Having just met the author made the read extra enjoyable.

I began to discover something of the place's history. Apparently the first group of houses I came across is called First Terrace and the second is called – no prizes for guessing correctly – Second Terrace. Believe it or not the house with the bay window once was *The Ship Hotel* and there was even a second hotel, *The Maxwell Arms* in Second Terrace. Why would a hamlet of only a couple of dozen houses need two hotels? The author's cottage in the lane, the one with the stone steps leading to a first floor front door, is appropriately known as *Upsteps Cottage*.

Sunderland Point developed as a port for Lancaster at the beginning of the eighteenth century importing cotton, sugar, rum and tobacco from the West Indies and timber, iron, flax, hemp and tar from the Baltic. Robert Gillow the famous Lancaster furniture maker imported mahogany from Barbados. Ships would tie up here to have their cargo transferred to lighters or carts. Boats were built here too, and there were warehouses, an anchor smithy, a block-makers and a rope works. No wonder they managed to support two hotels.

Walking around it is difficult to imagine the place as a bustling port. The most apt description I could give it now is a haven of peace. There is something honest and unpretentious about it. This is one place I will definitely be returning to.

A sentence from *The Story of Sunderland Point* is an appropriate one with which to end with.

'We hope you will enjoy a visit to Sunderland and that you will like the village, but even if you are unimpressed you will have to admit it is unusual.'

WEST BY NORTH

ISLE OF WALNEY

CUMBRIA

The Isle of Walney can be found off the end of what one local resident described to me disparagingly as the largest cul-de-sac in England. As well as splendid views of Morecambe Bay and the hills around the southern end of Lake Windermere, the journey down it provides some unusual sights.

Before reaching the end of the peninsula at Barrow-in-Furness you pass through the small town of Ulverston, famous for being the birthplace of Stan Laurel (there is a museum dedicated to him and his portly cinematic partner). Conspicuous on a hillside on the approach to the town is a monument in the form of a lighthouse, one and half miles from the sea at high tide and more than ten at low tide. The tower commemorates another of the town's noted former residents. As an explorer, geographer, Second Secretary to the Admiralty and promoter of Polar voyages, Sir John Barrow is remembered in places even more far flung than here, having named after him a Cape in the Antarctic and in the Arctic a Sound, a Strait, a Point and even a species of diving duck.

After passing through or round Barrow-in-Furness the Isle of Walney is reached by crossing Jubilee Bridge, which has a drawbridge section that opens to let ships pass along Walney Channel.

The histories of Walney and Barrow are inextricably linked. Cistercian monks from the twelfth century Furness Abbey, the impressive remains of which stand on the north side of Barrow, smelted iron on the island. Exploitation of the area's ore deposits in the nineteenth century led to Barrow becoming the largest iron and steel centre in the world, when it might have been more aptly described as Barrow-in-Furnace. Walney provides the shelter from the open sea that makes Barrow such a superb natural harbour and the shipbuilding industry that developed here alongside the iron and steel production is now Britain's biggest, with the largest covered shipbuilding hall in Europe.

A low lying reef on a north/south axis, Walney is ten miles long and varies in width from just a few hundred metres in the southern half, to about a mile in the north. A sandy beach runs the entire length of the west coast, backed by dunes in the north and an exposed layer of sand forming a low cliff in the south.

On my first visit to Walney, during the break in my encounters with Cleveleys, the tide was high and the beach covered by the sea. I spent an enjoyable time in warm summer sunshine discovering the island and did some preparatory work during which

I saw my first ever live badger. Knowing that later on in the life of these travels I would be passing nearby several times on my various journeys along the M6 motorway, I decided not to commit myself to a definitive painting at this stage, but to wait and see what a later visit would reveal.

Consequently, I was on Walney again 17 months later on a crisp and sunny November day, breaking a journey home from Scotland. This time I saw something a little more unusual than a badger on the way there.

Until then, I had thought that the camel I once saw grazing in a field off the A34 between Oxford and Bicester was about the strangest thing I had seen on my travels around Britain (bactrian or dromedary? I was too surprised to notice), but near a roundabout on the outskirts of Barrow, next to a field of common or garden Holsteins (or maybe they were Friesians) was a paddock occupied by two rhinoceros. Don't ask which sort they were, I was doing 30 mph at the time and concentrating on the traffic.

Glancing into the Walney Channel as I crossed the Jubilee Bridge I noticed that the tide was out, so headed straight for the beach. Here I found that a wide expanse of firm sand was exposed, interspersed with areas of rock, pools of stranded sea water edged by beds of large pebbles and a few scattered larger rocks encrusted in mussels.

I became captivated by the patterns the receding sea had made in the sand as it moved around and across the sand, rocks and pebbles, leaving areas of pronounced ripples round the edge of the pools and craters edged with fan-like patterns scooped out from around the larger rocks. All this was enhanced by the bright, low winter sunshine.

One could have filmed a walk across this beach and all sense of scale would have been lost. It could easily have given the impression of a river delta viewed from an aircraft, or even a dry continent seen from an orbiting spacecraft.

I spent most of this visit on the beach, having decided that as I was here to record the last landfall then this, temporarily, was it until the sea retuned to claim it.

With its large expanses of sand, dunes and areas of saltmarsh surrounding low lying pasture, much of it designated as National Nature Reserve, Walney is very much like the other places I have visited around Morecambe Bay. In fact its similarity to the rural landscape one crosses to reach Sunderland Point is remarkable. However, where man has made his mark on the island it is quite different.

During the second half of the nineteenth century, when it was in Lancashire, Barrow-in Furness became a boom town. In 1864, for instance, its population grew from just 300 to more than 8,000 and by 1881 it had reached 47,000. This growth, although rapid, was well planned and the town gives no impression that in those days it just 'grow'd like Topsy'.

The town's centre has wide boulevards, with squares at the major intersections that are overlooked by grand civic buildings. The terrace houses built for the steel and shipyard workers were good for their time, larger than normal for northern towns, with more space between the rows of houses and well ahead of almost anywhere in the country for the provision of lavatories. By 1906 the town was even using its refuse to generate electricity; advanced green thinking for its time.

By the end of the nineteenth century, however, the town was beginning to run out of space and the shipbuilding company Vickers created a subsidiary, The Isle of Walney Estates Company, to develop land for housing on the island. The result is Vickerstown,

54°04.8'N 3°15.0'W

Walney pasture with shipyard and Lake District beyond

a company estate of 1,000 houses built between 1900 and 1905 (added to later), very much in the mould of developments already underway at Port Sunlight by Lever Brothers and Bourneville by Cadburys. While not exactly a garden suburb like them (there was no need to create a rural atmosphere as they already had the real thing) it is unusual as an 'island suburb', possibly the only one of its kind in Britain.

Houses were built in a variety of styles and materials, with the layout following the natural contours of the undulating site. Some of the streets take their name from warships built at Barrow by Vickers, so there are a few unfortunate folk who have Vengeance Street as their address, but there are roads whose names convey more a sense of the place; Sandy Gap Lane is one I could live with.

Even in Vickerstown it is possible to come across the unexpected. Travelling along the main thoroughfare across the island, the almost exotic sounding Ocean Road, I passed a large open space between the houses where you might usually expect to find a park with formal flower beds and paths between avenues of trees, or maybe a playing field with goal posts, but this open space turned out to be neither of these. It was an area of tidal saltmarsh.

My immediate thought was for the safety of children growing up alongside such a potentially hazardous site, but they no doubt accept it as just another part of normal daily life. It will not be until they are older and more travelled that they will one day realise how unusual that was, maybe turning to a colleague one day and saying,

"In the town where I grew up, instead of a park at the end of our garden we had a saltmarsh."

To which the reply might be,

"Oh yes, and I supposed herds of wild animals roam thereabouts."

"Well, you're not going to believe this, but ..."

If you think you've seen it all, then come to Walney and be prepared for a surprise along the way.

WEST-NORTH-WEST

DUDDON SANDS
CUMBRIA

The River Duddon begins life in Wrynose Pass. The gathering waters falling off the slopes of Pike o'Blisco to the south-east of Bow Fell in the Cumbrian mountains flow south-west through Dunnerdale, entering the sea to the north of Barrow in Furness.

That modest 25 mile journey from fellside to the Irish Sea so inspired William Wordsworth in 1820 that he was moved to write a series of 34 sonnets about the river. Sonnet I introduces them:

> *...Pure flow the verse, pure, vigorous, free and bright,*
> *For Duddon, long-loved Duddon, is my theme!*

Three times I travelled down the single track road near Dalton in Furness to the National Trust's car park by the shore at Sandscale Haws dunes, crossing them to stand on the broad sands of Duddon's estuary in search of my inspiration.

The first visit was after a wet drive from Cleveleys. Pouring rain and the gloomy greyness of a June afternoon which should have known better concealed any distant views there might have been and I found little of interest. Hardly anything could be seen on the far shore and the view on my side was of a receding tide gradually exposing more sand, the water's edge marked by a seemingly infinite strip of scummy foam that shuddered in the wind, like an everlasting quivering head of Guinness.

That evening the rain stopped and I made my second visit. What a transformation had taken place. The sparkling sea was slowly returning to regain the estuary and a rich and heavy sky filled with clouds in many layers hung almost motionless over the Lake District's southern fells, hinting at the position of the evening sun. Instantly I knew that this would be the moment, a view that could surely not be bettered. Wordsworth's description of Duddon's estuary, in Sonnet XXXII, fits the scene perfectly.

> *Not hurled precipitous from steep to steep;*
> *Lingering no more 'mid flower-enamelled lands*
> *And blooming thickets; nor by rocky bands*
> *Held; but in radiant progress toward the Deep*
> *Where mightiest rivers into powerless sleep*
> *Sink, and forget their nature – now expands*
> *Majestic Duddon, over smooth flat sands*
> *Gliding in silence with unfettered sweep!*
> *Beneath an ampler sky a region wide*
> *Is opened round him: - hamlets, towers and towns,*
> *And blue-topped hills, behold him from afar;...*

54°10.2'N 3°13.8'W

The next day dawned bright and sunny and I thought I deserved some time spent sketching in pleasant conditions for a change. Quite sure that the previous evening's spectacle was beyond anything I was likely to witness again I had the luxury of daubing without the necessity to produce something usable later.

A good vantage point was eventually found on top of one of the dunes. Sandscale Haws dunes are a National Nature Reserve owned by the National Trust. *Haws* is a Norse word for hills and is most apt here, they are like the Lake District in miniature. The name Sandscale too is Scandinavian in origin; *sandra* meaning beach and *skali* hut. The Haws are a living history of dunes, with examples from every stage in the life cycle of the sand dune from small wind-blown accumulations of sand just above the high water line and dunes with the first signs of colonisation by marram grass, to fully fledged, stable inland dunes anchored by a covering mat of permanent grassland.

The dunes are home to Britain's rarest amphibian. Of the national population of natterjack toads, fifteen per cent – hundreds of them – live here, hiding in burrows during the day and hunting for insects and gathering at their spawning pools at night, just like teenagers really. A pool has been created near to the car park so that visitors can see the toads and hear their call without disturbing those who prefer to use the natural pools.

The dune system covers 282 hectares and to preserve their ecological balance the Trust maintains a now rare traditional grazing practice that began here in the twelfth century. Beef cattle graze all the year round and from spring to autumn they are joined by flocks of Herdwick and Swaledale ewes and lambs. Small areas have been fenced off to prevent grazing, thus demonstrating the detrimental changes that would be brought about if the practice ceased.

From my elevated vantage point I could look out across the varied dunescape, but the view north across Duddon Sands was especially wonderful. The air was much clearer than the previous evening. The small town of Millom on the opposite shore stood conspicuous in the morning sunshine and behind it the 600 metres high Black Combe, the one prominent peak on that previous occasion, was now joined by some of the more distant southern Lakeland hills; Ulpha Fell, Harter Fell, Scafell and the Old Man of Coniston, a name that always brings to mind that writer and illustrator of the essential Lakeland guides Alfred Wainwright.

To the east, on the nearby hills south of the Duddon the blades of a wind farm rotated slowly and silently in a westerly breeze, the only significant movement in an otherwise still scene.

Sitting in the soft sand with a sketchbook in my lap, palette in my left hand and a pot of water resting in the sand at my right side I began painting.

Sketching progressed nicely. For a while I was the sole occupant of this corner of Cumbria, but eventually I was joined by a family group enjoying a walk in the warm sunshine on a morning out from Barrow in Furness. They comprised an elderly couple with their two grandchildren, one of each of about nine and eleven years of age and two border collies, a mother and daughter of indeterminate vintage.

I had a conversation with the older couple about why this is not one of my regular painting spots;

"Do you live far from here then?"

"About 300 miles."

I showed the children how I use the materials, prompted by one of those 'Cor, have you just done that, mister?' remarks.

The impromptu lesson came to a sudden end when the canine couple in the party became over inquisitive and one of them kicked over my pot of water, accompanied by an apparently well rehearsed chorus of, "Oh dear, sorry about that, she tends to be a bit clumsy, she's deaf and partially sighted you know."

Their feeling of guilt was assuaged when I replied "That's OK, at least it will give me something different to write about. It's definitely a first for me."

So, to commemorate the event, for the first time I am showing an unfinished piece, started by Collyer and finished by collie...

Duddon Estuary – low Tide

NORTH-WEST BY WEST

CORSEWALL POINT
DUMFRIES & GALLOWAY

The Rhinns of Galloway might sound like a late night Radio 4 alternative comedy sit-com, a sort of McArchers on acid maybe, but in fact it's that hammer-head shaped peninsula on the north side of the Solway Firth.

It is border country without a land border with England, but well fortified nevertheless if the number of castles marked on the Ordnance Survey map are anything to go by. None, as far as I have been able to ascertain, are home to the Lord of the Rhinns.

Rhinns, by the way, is from the Gaelic for a point or promontory. Here are a few tips from my limited understanding of Gaelic. Vowels are short, unless they have an accent over them, in which case they are long. You might come unstuck with vowel combinations as they're not always what they seem. Occasionally a second vowel preceding a consonant might only be there to balance the same vowel coming after it, and is silent. Sometimes you will find a silent (more or less) pair of consonants, as with the *bh* in Steornabhagh (Stornoway), but if they begin a word they would be pronounced as a *v*, as would *mh*.

Most importantly, the emphasis is always on the first syllable. Remember that and you can't go wrong.

My second foray into Scotland on these travels was to the north of this peninsula. It is a gently rolling landscape, a patchwork of green fields separated by dry-stone walls, with the occasional small area of woodland; a landscape that's more typical of northern England than Scotland.

The narrow road to Corsewall Point meanders out between the fields, passing the occasional white-painted farmhouse, more characteristically Scottish in appearance, and the remains of the fifteenth century Corsewall Castle. It is a pretty drive, with overhanging trees and plenty of gorse to add a splash of vibrant colour. The sea is often visible, looking like it is just beyond the next wall, but there always seems to be yet another bend as the road gradually becomes a lane and then little more than a farm track. There's only the occasional sign to reassure that you'll be there soon.

The journey ends at a meadow of tussocky grass about 10 metres above sea level. Towards the sea, the grass gives way to lichen covered rocks that fall away, becoming darker where they are constantly washed and scoured by the waves before eventually disappearing into the water.

I arrived late one April afternoon in glorious sunshine, the low sun sparkling on the water. Out to sea the only landmark was to the north, the blue silhouette of Ailsa Craig, that 340 metre high rounded mound of granite, like a giant muffin, instantly recognisable to those who have ever seen golf from Turnberry on television.

The weather forecast for the next couple of days was not that encouraging, so I was grateful to have an hour or so of evening sunshine in which to get some useful work under my belt. As I was about to leave, a ferry emerged from Loch Ryan to the east, rounding the headland and setting off across the North Channel en route from Stranraer to Belfast. The ferry's appearance emphasised the fact that I was almost surrounded by sea and for a while I was left with the feeling of being on an island, which somehow made sense at the time.

The next morning was unexpectedly bright and breezy. Visibility had improved greatly and I became aware for the first time that Corsewall Point was not the isolated spot it had seemed the previous evening. It is, in fact, encircled by land and I was surprised at how close it all looked.

Behind and a little to the left of Ailsa Craig could be seen the still snow-streaked peaks of the Isle of Arran, some of them 30 miles away. Then further round to the north west and a little closer was the southern end of the Kintyre peninsula and to the west, was half the coastline of Northern Ireland. The nearest point is a mere 23 miles off. What a panorama!

Suddenly, instead of being remote and on the fringe, it felt like Corsewall Point was at the centre and significant.

My immediate surroundings looked very much as they had the day before, although the sea was noticeably more choppy as it thundered and sprayed up the fissures in the rocks, at one moment deep dark gullies, the next hissing channels of churning white foam.

Over the land, pied wagtails flitted energetically from rock to rock, a pair of early swallows occasionally swooped close by and a kestrel hunted for its lunch. In sheltered crevices between the rocks stonecrop and thrift rustled and bobbed in the breeze. Just offshore was the main flight-path to the gannets' feeding ground and for several hours they passed low over the sea in groups of three or four, alternately flapping then gliding in unison.

Although many hundreds of people pass by this spot every day on the Northern Ireland ferries, a relatively modest few make the journey down the lane, as I had, with a purpose. Some no doubt come here to watch the birds, walk along the shore, or just to take in the stupendous view, but most of them come to visit the one feature of this spot I have so far failed to mention; Corsewall Point Lighthouse.

Perched on the rocks close to the shoreline it is one of Scotland's oldest lights, built in 1815–16 by Robert Stevenson, the father of Scotland's lighthouse system and its family of builders, and grandfather of the author Robert Louis Stevenson. It's an impressive group of buildings in the Northern Lighthouse Board's livery of white with detailing picked out in a yellow ochre (the Board's current paint supplier call it oasis, more universally it's known as BS 08 C 35, but I'm sure you didn't really want to know that).

The 34 metre high tapering rough stone lantern tower is particularly fine, being divided into five sections by smooth string-courses. The lower section is topped with a projecting castelated walkway and the top one nicely detailed with blind quatrefoils. The lighthouse keepers' house is an attractive flat roofed

55º0.4'N 5º09.4'W

lichen and thrift

navigational aids have put paid to that, so guests can sleep soundly at night whatever the weather.

The elegant surroundings are nicely nautical; naturally.

My appetite was certainly whetted, and I only had a coffee over a chat with the owner.

On working trips like this I try to stay somewhere that's small and 'local' where I can meet people who have an 'at the coal face' knowledge of the area. That way I usually find answers and explanations for the occasional sights and events that need some clarification.

On this occasion I had

block with prominent quoins and tall chimney stacks.

However, there is something almost unique about this lighthouse beyond its architectural splendour and dramatic setting that gives it its particular appeal for visitors. Although still functioning as a lighthouse, albeit automatically like all the others in Britain, this is also the Corsewall Lighthouse Hotel.

Now what could be more romantic than that?

Sadly there are no circular rooms as the tower still belongs to the Lighthouse Board, but thankfully the foghorn is no longer in operation, modern electronic

B&B just down the road at Clachan Farm and it was one of my most enjoyable experiences yet, another good reason to make the journey out here. There, I was able to find an answer to something that had puzzled me on my various journeys out to Corsewall Point. Why are there a dozen or so dead moles tied to the fence at the side of the road? Well, apparently the local mole catcher is so proud of his success rate that he displays his trophies to advertise his expertise. I'm sure you didn't want to know that either, but it all adds to the local colour, which is, if you remember, oasis; quite appropriate really.

NORTH-WEST

CORNAIG, TIREE
ARGYLL & BUTE

Tiree? Where's that? That's most peoples' response.

It is small and to the west of Mull, the most outer of the Inner Hebrides islands and if the name sounds familiar it's probably because it is one of the coastal stations on the Shipping Forecast. That's why I'd been before. It made quite an impression on me first time round and after eight years my memory of that visit was still vivid, so I was looking forward to this second trip very much.

I am not passionately in love with Tiree, but I have grown very fond of it.

It's not ravishingly beautiful like Skye and it doesn't brazenly show off its cleavage like Jura (there are no Paps of Tiree), but it has a gentle and homely 'island next door' charm that is irresistible. If I could adopt an island this would be the one; somehow I feel protective towards it.

Tiree is a meadow in the sea; a low, lush and lovely sliver of machair dotted with cottages. If you're wondering about machair, it is a Gaelic word for a low lying meadow produced when lime-rich shell-sand is blown off the shore over naturally acid soil. Globally rare, it is found only in the Hebrides, the Northern Isles and the west coast of Ireland. It is green for most the year but bursts into a fragrant and colourful carpet of flowers in the summer.

Tiree is ten and a half miles long and between five and a half and half a mile wide. Physically it is almost featureless with three-quarters of the land below 20 metres. Consequently the sky and the weather (particularly the wind) dominate. I have been here when the sky has been grey and filled with rain that elsewhere would cast a depressing gloom over everything, but here there is still a strange eye-squinting brightness. Perhaps they could use that in their publicity; Tiree – never a dull moment. If global warming is for real and it leads to relentlessly rising sea levels I cannot imagine what sort of future the island has, but there is the remote possibility that it could become uninhabited before then anyway.

One hundred and fifty years ago the island had a population of four and a half thousand, today it is somewhere in the mid seven hundreds, with almost two thirds of them past retirement age. At present the population is described as 'steady', there is still a slight decline and if they eventually get down to around four hundred they would be at a level thought to be unsustainable, but the decline shows signs of levelling off, so things may not get that desperate.

56°31.3'N 6°54.0'W

This depopulation has been the result of voluntary emigration over a long period of time. Even when the population was at its peak it was thought to be unsustainable and the Duke of Argyll, whose family have owned Tiree since 1675, paid for the passage (three pounds ten shillings) of those who wanted to leave and start a new life in Canada. One thousand took up the offer between 1847 and 1851. The team that look after the archives on the island estimate that around the world there are 38,000 people of Tiree descent and they refer to this scattered family as the Tiree diaspora.

The problem, as always in communities like this, is the lack of enough work to keep everyone gainfully occupied and interested and, amongst the young, the sense that everything is happening elsewhere.

One solution would be to introduce work that could be done anywhere and to that end their saviour could come in the form of the humming beige box. At the time of my visit Argyll and Bute Council were preparing to provide every household on Tiree (and on twelve other islands for which they are responsible) with a free computer, complete with printer and internet access. Some on the island see this as having limitless possibilities that will bring dramatic change; electronically they could be anywhere.

On this visit my attention was focussed on an area of the north side of the island. The signs at the side of the road proclaim that you are entering Cornaig, although it is not quite as simple as that. There are two neighbouring communities that bear that prefix, Cornaigbeg and Cornaigmore, and there is also a Cornaig Beach, or Tràigh Chornaig. As with many other Tiree place-names they are a mixture of Gaelic and Norse; Cornaig is Norse for Corn Bay, and the suffixes are Gaelic, bheag – small and mhor – large.

The Cornaigs are two of thirty-four crofting townships on the island. In most instances the townships are a loose grouping of crofts, with many of their buildings in the island's vernacular, single storey and white painted (and also with Scotland's highest concentration of traditional thatched buildings – twelve in all). For once Mother Nature has a rival, it is these groups of buildings set among meadows of grazing sheep and cattle that gives the island it's beauty.

Although between them the townships on the south side of the island have just about all of the facilities; the ferry terminal, bank, post office, grocery stores, butcher's shop, doctor's surgery, garages, fire tender and one-man police station, Cornaigmore has the one that everyone has continually returned to over the generations, the island's school.

As you can imagine the school's population is not huge. Even though they educate all of the island's children right up until they are 18 there was, at the time of my visit, only a total of 52 secondary and 64 primary pupils. The pupil to teacher ratio is something most mainland teachers would only dream of, averaging out to less than four and a half pupils per teacher.

On the whole this serves the pupils well. If any of them need extra help or attention it can be provided, but sometimes there is a down side as keeping the dynamic of a lesson going in very small classes can be difficult. In some subjects children from more than one year will be taught together.

At primary level parents can elect to have their children educated in either Gaelic or English and the split is about equal, although at home they are more likely to use English. At secondary level most of the resources are in English so there isn't so much choice.

On the whole the children are pretty much the same mix you would expect anywhere and as such they reach the end of their time here with the same aspirations. In some cases that will involve leaving the island for a mainland university, or agriculture college where there is a specialist crofting course (although fewer than a third of the island's 286 crofts are now worked the traditional way).

Close to the school a stile gives access to the fenced off area of machair between Cornaigmore and the beach. Crossing it to the dunes in one of those 'this is the life' muses I came to the conclusion that one of Tiree's greatest assets is its silence; it hits you as soon as you step outdoors. Admittedly there is nearly always the sound of the wind blowing through your ears, but you soon become accustomed to that and most of the time all you can hear is birdsong; probably a skylark or some oystercatchers, the occasional curlew and something I rarely hear or see back home, but is quite common here, lapwing. It is absolutely wonderful.

A fence runs the length of the dunes to stop unwary grazing animals from falling the five metres down onto the beach. Fortunately, I found that a tiny dune had developed over a section of fence allowing me to climb over gracefully; Mother Nature's stile.

More than a third of Tiree's forty-six miles of coastline is beach, with this one and eleven others longer than half a mile. On the beach my only companions were a couple of hares; there are no rabbits on the island and they don't want any. The local joke is (and to appreciate it you need to know that hares don't dig, they live in shallow depressions) if they had rabbits the island would sink.

White sand, turquoise sea, clear blue sky, it is almost tropical. Almost.

Tiree is often the sunniest place in Britain in May. The mean annual temperature is only one degree less than southern England's and the difference between summer and winter is just 8.5°C, while in southern England it is 14°C. The lowest temperature ever recorded here is only –6.7°C.

During my stay I met several people who had moved here from the mainland and were glad they did. In every case they gave me the same reason; "quality of life".

cattle feeders at Cornaigmore

NORTH-WEST BY NORTH

SGARASTA BHEAG, SOUTH HARRIS
WESTERN ISLES

You occasionally hear or read of somewhere described as being in 'the interior' of a country, implying that it is somewhere remote, wild or inaccessible, or all three. The interior is a place where you have to hack your way through dense undergrowth, risk being eaten by wolves or an army of insects, or have heroically to carry your camel on your shoulders after it has collapsed from exhaustion.

South Harris has just such an interior. You have to cross it to get from the ferry terminal at Tarbert, which is on the east coast, to Sgarasta Bheag (Scaristabeg) on the west. It's the living (a rather inappropriate adjective here) embodiment of the word rugged.

After about eight miles of this grey, glacier ground landscape, liberally strewn haphazardly with gigantic jagged boulders, there comes into view the first sighting of the west coast. Beyond vivid green machair, a deep ultramarine sea breaks onto a beach of near-white sand in a crash of dazzling silver spray; it's like a mirage.

From the township of Seilebost the single track coast road sweeps left then right, over headlands and round bays in a roughly south-westerly direction; through the townships of Horgabost, Borgh (Borve), Sgarasta Bhor (Scaristavore) and finally Sgarasta

Bheag, after which it starts to leave the coast and head south-east. Along that nine mile stretch the best view is always behind you and it was that I wanted to see from Sgarasta Bheag's dunes.

They appeared to be fenced off, but I found a field gate that gave me access. In Scotland there is no law of trespass, so walkers have the right to roam. Coming from England I find this difficult to get used to and felt hesitant at just wandering in. As luck would have it the farmer came my way in hot pursuit of a stray ewe. My car seemed to be a sufficient bar to make it hesitate, enabling him to grab it and heave it over the fence as if it was a sack of potatoes.

He seemed quite happy with my intention and off I strolled.

He hadn't warned me that the dunes were home to a herd of cattle, some of which had impressive sets of horns. I tried to act nonchalantly and said hello, which elicited no response, I'm glad to say. I guess they only understood Gaelic.

The scale of the dunes here is impressive and they provided the perfect elevated vantage point from which to take in views of both Sgarasta Bheag and what I really wanted to see from here, the mountains of North Harris across the Sound of Taransay.

The further north you go along this shore the whiter the shell-sand appears, the finer the grains, the lighter the colour. In sunshine it is dazzling. I reckon it must be illuminated from underground. It glows even when it is cloudy or in a heavy shower. A more appropriate greeting for this scene would have been aloha.

This is the view and this is the life, I thought to myself. At moments like this, I feel guilty that I am able to enjoy such splendour as part of my work when so many people spend their days chained to a desk or on a production line. To know that this is Britain is heart-warming. An hour of this taken once a year should be available on the NHS, we'd all be so much healthier for it.

I think I have become addicted and taken an overdose.

Just to the north over the boundary in Sgarasta Bhor the dunes and machair are used by the Isle of Harris Golf Club, where you can take out life membership for a very modest £150. If you fancy a round, green fees are a mere £10 a day (juniors £2.50) and you pop the money into an honesty box. Nick Faldo did this once, signing the banknote before he fed it through the slot. They had it framed and now play an annual competition for it. It's a nine hole course; I caught up with a twosome about to tee off and asked if people wanting the full eighteen holes could go round twice. They thought for a moment then replied with a smile "Well, you could do that, but it rarely stops raining long enough".

Sgarasta Bheag is a small community stretching along the road for six passing places. On the seaward side there is a small collection of houses, mostly single storey, a range of stone barns and a pair of corrugated iron sheds that were once used for weaving Harris tweed. Facing them across the road is a Post Office, the Church of Scotland church and cemetery that also serve the neighbouring townships and the former Georgian manse, now Scarista House where they do luxurious B&B and magnificent evening meals.

The handful of townships along this coastal strip are on land that had for a century been a deer shooting estate, until it was bought in the mid 1930s by the Scottish Board of Agriculture. They divided it into crofts, reinstating the system of land use that had been swept aside when the estate was created. I stayed in a croft house in Horgabost, which the present crofter helped his father build in the late 1940s when he took the croft over from the Board. They have twelve hectares of land and graze a hundred sheep on the machair.

It might seem idylic to an outsider but, like the farmers I met on Sanday, for most it involves having one or more part time jobs in addition to looking after the animals to keep it all together and survive.

The crofting system is highly regulated through an office in Inverness. I have heard crofts described as parcels of land entirely surrounded by regulations. For instance, they are often passed down through the family, as this one was; if the parents wanted to continue living in a house after a son or daughter has taken on the land, permission would have be sought to de-croft the land on which the house stood. I saw just such a notice, in effect a planning application, taped to a telephone box on Tiree.

Whatever the merits or not of the system it has protected the environment here from inappropriate development and that's one of the attractions for visitors, giving the impression that life here has hardly changed in fifty years, which is not the case at all.

57°49.7'N 7°04.2'W

Sgarasta Bheag Sun loungers

Some crofters are involved in the weaving of Harris tweed. To qualify as such and receive the famous orb trade mark the fabric must be made from 100% Scottish wool that has been died, spun and finished in the Outer Hebrides. Originally the wool came from local blackface sheep, which produced a heavy course tweed, but now it's spun from other wools for a softer, lighter fabric (today blackface wool is more likely to be used in carpets). The weaving too has to be done in the Outer Hebrides and must be hand woven by the islanders at their own homes.

This is still done on manual looms, usually in small sheds, which you will see at the side of the road as you travel round these outer isles.

The weavers are all freelance and are likely to have learned the craft from a parent. Most will be supplying cloth to one or more mills that will provide them with the yarn and dictate the weight, pattern and colours of the tweed they are making.

I spoke to one who makes his entire living from weaving what soon takes on a capital letter and becomes Harris Tweed. Unusually he develops, with the help of his wife, his own patterns and colours, working closely with garment manufacturers that he supplies direct, giving them something more exclusive and allowing him to be more creative. When tweed is fashionable it is a case of burning the midnight oil to keep up with the demand. This may seem a less steady way of working, but as he put it, "It makes life more interesting".

That comment had a familiar ring to it. For once I, the freelance artist and writer, had found someone with whom I could more closely identify.

150

NORTH-NORTH-WEST

BADLUARACH

HIGHLAND

Badluarach. Bad–loo–a–rack, that's how I'd pronounce it, but what do I know? I'm a Sassenach. Badloo–arack; it can't be that straight forward, it never is. If a ferry sailed from here no doubt we would know it well and it would just trip off the tongue as easily as Steornabhagh.

Actually, a ferry does sail from here, in a way, but I'll come to that later.

Between my two visits to Badluarach I stayed overnight at *The Sheiling*, an immaculate and highly recommended guesthouse at Achgarve, a short and breathtakingly scenic drive away on the far side of Gruinard (pronounced Grin-yard) Bay. Annabell, who runs it, grew up close by so was able to give me the definitive pronunciation; Bad–loorack. Close. Apparently it means the clump of rushes.

You will find Badluarach on the Ordnance Survey Landranger Map 19. Each of these masterpieces covers an area 25 by 25 miles. To give some idea of the extent of that on the ground, Manchester fits comfortably into the eastern half of map 109, which also covers Wilmslow, Warrington and Rochdale, number 196 covers Southampton, Portsmouth and the whole of the Isle of Wight. Look at number 19 and you will find a mass of tightly packed contour

lines and just two, yes only two, A roads, one of those making only a brief appearance in the top right hand corner where you will also find the only town, Ullapool (population a modest 2,000 or so).

To find Badluarach, flip open the map, and grabbing the key section next to 'public rights of way' pull it open to reveal the top half as far as Gruinard Bay. From Ullapool follow Loch Broom out into The Minch to the top edge of the sheet, turn south round the end of the Scoraig peninsula headland by Cailleach Head and you are into Little Loch Broom. Badluarach is on the south shore at the seaward end, between the third and fourth fold from your right hand.

On the ground it's not that easy, especially in November.

My companion for the first part of my journey there was Libby Purves with her *Midweek* programme, coming out of the ether on a faint and crackly Radio 4 long-wave signal. No sooner had "My guests this week …" passed her lips than I ran into an arctic blizzard that cut me down to a crawl until, magically, it stopped when she said "my guests next week will include …"

Fortunately, being built in Sweden, my car is designed to take such things in its stride, with

Rayburn-like heater settings – simmer, bake and roast and I still managed the journey in reasonable time, if arriving a little later than anticipated. I found my destination by leaving the coast road at Badcaul and taking the single track road that runs for two and a half miles parallel with the south shore of Little Loch Broom, 70 metres above and a about 400 metres away from the waters of the loch.

After passing through a Forestry Commission conifer plantation that straddles the road I saw the first few buildings of Badluarach's scattered community.

The landscape to my left was mostly a gentle hillside of tan-coloured peat moorland, a rough grassland with heather and liberally scattered with stones varying in size from footballs to pillows. To my right, on the loch side of the road were a number of fenced off fields of coarse grass from which the larger stones had been cleared. An empty sheep pen stood in the corner of one field close to the road. Along the shore of the loch there was an extensive area of natural birch woodland.

Badluarach's buildings are a mixture of small Victorian houses, typically single storey with dormers, and a few modern bungalows. On the loch side of the road were the remains of a number of small croft houses. Some looked like they might still be in use for storage, but some looked as if they were abandoned long ago; just a gable end or two and a section of wall where it was just possible to make out the former location of a window or doorway.

There was not a soul to be seen, but sheep wandered across the road oblivious to my presence.

I passed a telephone box and eventually came to a post box where there was a junction, with a lane down to the shore of the loch. I turned down here. At the bottom there were a couple of boats on trailers, a number of vans and cars and a large shed where, through the open door I could see some oilskins hanging up. A drift of sleet against the shed indicated that polar conditions struck here too. The lane ended at a slipway and it was here that I parked.

The view from this spot was fabulous.

At this point Little Loch Broom is about a mile wide. The far side looked remarkably like this one. There was another scattered community, Scoraig, with the lower slopes similarly fenced off and houses, just as in Badluarach, surrounded by dry stone walls or bounded by conifers to give them some protection from the wind which spun the blades of a small generator at one of the houses. There was also a slipway.

This view however had one dominant feature, which I knew I would have to paint the moment I pulled on the handbrake, Beinn Ghobhlach (a soft gargle, followed by olack). At a mere 635 metres it ranks a lowly seven hundred and sixty ninth among Scotland's many great peaks, but what it lacks in stature it more than makes up for in appearance, with two buttress–like peaks linked by a crescent shaped ridge forming a corrie. I appeared to have the most perfectly placed seat to enjoy the view, which I did for nearly four hours.

For a while the only movement was the surface of the loch, ruffled by a strong northerly wind that moved heavy grey clouds rapidly across the sky. My only companions were a robin, which scratched around at the edge of the track, a hooded crow on look-out duty on a fence post and a buzzard that circled above the shoreline.

As the afternoon drew towards sunset the sky began to clear a little and the odd small break in the

57°54.3'N 5°23.2'W

looking back
Badmarach

isn't a proper road along their side of the loch. Apparently they have been offered one, but turned it down. They obviously value their isolation, the ferry being their link with the outside world. The post boat only makes one round trip from that inaccessible side so you can go over to Scoraig, but you would have to wait a couple of days before you could get back.

Overnight we had sleet, hail and snow. I returned to the slipway to see that the view had not changed dramatically. Beinn Ghobhlach had been given a dusting of snow, but not the comprehensive coating I had expected and hoped for. A strong wind buffeted the car as I watched showers pass across the loch, wiping the mountain of its details and turning it into a pale golden grey silhouette. The wind blew clouds of snow off Beinn Ghobhlach's corrie into the air and it swirled around like smoke from a bonfire caught in a whirlwind.

I understand the views from up there are quite spectacular … but next time maybe. I was simmering nicely.

At eleven fifteen the post van arrived. The postman got a grey mail sack out of the back and locked it in a concrete box the size of a small coalbunker. He gave me a nod and a smile as if to say 'you're in for a long wait, mate' and drove off. I assumed that was going to be today's performance, so I hit the road myself before it disappeared beneath the snow.

clouds allowed isolated patches of sunlight to scud across Beinn Ghobhlach's slopes. This came to a dramatic finale when on one spine tingling occasion the peaks alone were brilliantly illuminated as if to say 'and now, the moment you have been waiting for, the star of today's show…' I gave it a standing ovation, but there was still no one else in sight to share the performance with me.

Before leaving I called in at the village stores and post office for a fix of dark chocolate. They appeared to sell almost everything, and if they don't have what you want they will try to get it for you. If you have stayed around here and enjoyed something peculiarly local, they will even post it to you.

I asked them if a ferry ever ran from the slipway as one was shown on the OS map. They informed me that a post boat comes over from Scoraig on Mondays, Wednesdays and Fridays, because there

154

NORTH BY WEST

FARR

HIGHLAND

It seems somehow fitting that the final point on my travels should be the farthest away, on the mainland – or at least, from that soggy hillside above Dunsop Bridge where this journeying began, and how appropriate that it should be named Farr.

A straight line from Brown Syke Moss to Farr passes through the centre of Edinburgh, which isn't even half way and could not be more different from those starting and finishing points. My journey was to be more circuitous and less populous, involving a drive round Scotland's top left corner. The former county of Sutherland, now amalgamated into Highland, was somewhere I had not visited before and I had been looking forward with great anticipation to seeing it.

It seemed appropriate too that this journey should involve travelling across just about the most wild and desolate country I have ever seen in Britain, as if to emphasise the fact that I was about to arrive at the point where the land came to an end. Beyond that it's just the wild Atlantic and, eventually, the Arctic ice. Would I find a sign that read 'this is as Farr as you can go'?

Two hundred years ago the land away from the coastal fringe would not have been as sparsely populated as it appears now. With the look of a barren and boggy wasteland, once called Britain's Serengeti by David Bellamy, the bleak high moors are not likely to have seen any permanent settlement. The relatively lush straths, like Strathnaver that meets the sea at Torrisdale Bay just to the west of Farr, were well populated. In those days the parish of Farr supported three times the number it does now.

Though not an idyllic life, people somehow managed to survive by growing such crops as potatoes and barley in the valley bottoms while their livestock grazed on enclosed pasture and over the hillsides. The people would have lived in conditions that today would be considered primitive, in single room buildings that relied on turf roofs to keep the weather out, and the warmth of the cattle that shared their homes for central heating.

This ancient way of life came to an end when the Duke of Sutherland (an Englishman known as The Leviathan of Wealth) decided that he could make more money by evicting his tenants (15,000 in all) and allowing their land to be grazed by his newly acquired flocks of Cheviot sheep. This is an animal twice the size Mother Nature originally intended,

producing more wool and mutton per animal than other breeds, to clothe and feed the rapidly growing populations of the lowland towns and cities.

Those who manage to see this as a less than shameful episode would no doubt say that the tenants were not totally dispossessed, merely relocated on the coast, in villages like Bettyhill and on the headlands at Strathy, Armadale and Farr.

Here they were given small allotments of about half to three quarters of a hectare and were expected to be self sufficient in food while somehow making a living from fishing or quarrying. The paucity of the soil and the lack of a safe anchorage made the success of this exercise from the tenants point of view unlikely. It proved to be so.

However, that pattern of post-clearance settlements, with isolated houses sited on their individual plots of land is still evident at places like Farr.

Off the Durness to Thurso road immediately to the east of Bettyhill the small community at Farr is strung out for over a mile along a narrow lane that clings to an undulating hillside, ending abruptly at a cliff top crash barrier that has a 50 metre drop into the sea beyond it.

After my journey across miles of empty moorland overflowing in browns, russets and greys, the landscape seen from Farr was, by contrast, overwhelmingly green.

I was fortunate to have been here when the weather systems crossing the country were bringing clear, if cold, air from the north-west, providing bright sunshine and good visibility. From the cliff top there was a wonderful twelve-mile view of the islands and headlands along the coast to the west and inland to the peaks around the Munro Ben Clebrig, more than twenty miles away.

Occasionally on my travels, particularly in Scotland, I have one of those 'I could live with a view like this' thoughts and it happened here. I have been unable to decide if living on the coast, having it there all the time, would diminish some of its magic. Is it the infrequency of my visits that keeps it fresh and enjoyable?

Perhaps now was the time to give this some more serious thought, for as I stood and soaked up this scene I noticed that the house almost at the cliff edge, which enjoys this splendid view, was for sale. It looked like my sort of house. At times like this it's easy to become misty eyed and unrealistic, but I phoned the agents for the details anyway. It even had a study, which had that sea view – the agents called it stunning and for once they were right – but would I get any work done? Wouldn't I spend all my time looking out of the window? More importantly, could I cope with the isolation? This really was Farr from the madding crowd.

Would you believe it, that house was valued at little more than a Southwold beach hut.

There is more to Farr than this post-clearance community. There is also Farr Bay, a beautiful secluded beach nestling between Bettyhill's and Farr's rocky headlands.

I arrived there the following morning, early enough for the beach still to be in the shadow cast by the dunes that back the smooth sands. I had not been the first person there that morning, two sets of tracks indicated that someone had given a dog an early morning walk, and I soon discovered that I was sharing the sands with another occupant, who was probably not there out of choice.

A grey seal pup had become stranded beyond the area being washed by the breakers. I could not tell if

58°32.8'N 4°13.1'W

the tide was rising or falling, so had no idea how long it might have been there. It did not appear to be distressed, but was fairly inactive and aware of my presence.

I kept my distance and was wondering what to do when a teenage girl walking a Welsh collie appeared. She informed me that it had been there the previous afternoon and she had called the SSPCA to inform them. They had said that its mother might be around and could have left it while she had gone off to feed and so might return for it. If it was still there the following morning she should call them again and they would come out to rescue it.

We stayed with the seal awaiting their arrival. A couple of surfers appeared and came over to have a look. They were on a surfing safari round the north

Farr Bay rescue

coast, the north-west wind being just the right direction and strength to create perfect conditions for them in the bay here. I asked them if they had travelled far and they said about 700 miles, from Trowbridge. "Trowbridge!" I exclaimed, "I live only 15 miles from there."

The SSPCA team arrived, managed to pass a sheet under the seal to lift it and bundled it into an extra large plastic cat/dog basket. I automatically went into book research mode and began quizzing them about it.

They thought that it looked well nourished, obviously fed in the last day or two. It still had its off-white fluffy coat indicating that it was less than four weeks old and that it didn't swim here as it needs to shed the coat before it can do that. Along the coast there is a big seal colony on Eilean nan Ròn – Seal Island – and it is likely that it had been swept off the rocks there by a wave and carried to Farr Bay on the current.

They were going to put it on the Scrabster to Stromness Ferry to be collected at the other end by someone from the Orkney Seal Rescue Centre on South Ronaldsay. There it would probably be given liquid antibiotics – they suspected it had lungworm as its breathing was not as good as it should be – fed on milk, fish soup and eventually fish solids, then released into the wild.

Curious about my interest, I explained to them why I was there and that I could immortalise this moment in print, to which they replied "In that case we will name it after you."

After that, four of us grabbed a corner each and carried Peter over the dunes to their van in time to catch the midday sailing to Stromness.

At Orkney Seal Rescue, I later learned, Peter was put into a tank on his own for a couple of days to allow him to settle down and become acquainted with his new environment. He was then moved into their largest tank with another grey seal pup called Kenris, with whom he interacted extremely well. Peter shed his coat and they both made excellent progress, taking fish from the water and eventually getting their weight up to over 30 kilos.

During my contacts with Orkney Seal Rescue I also learned another peculiarity of our 'common' language. At this end of our islands the word for a seal, both grey and common, is selkie. This I discovered when I queried their email address selkiesave@aol.com (use it if you would like to help them).

Peter had set a seal on my amazing journeying the length and breadth of Britain. He was tagged with a microchip and returned to the wild on the island of Burray. For ten minutes or so he explored amongst the seaweed and rocks before disappearing into deeper water to join the other seals in the area. Aah!

ACKNOWLEDGEMENTS

I have had a wonderful time working on this book. I can thank my publisher Allan Brunton-Reed for the idea and Chris Beetles, who handles my paintings, for giving me the encouragement to go ahead with it. Their support and belief in my work keeps me going and helps maintain my standards, I am grateful to them both.

My family and close friends are very supportive. It is their belief and continued interest in my work that inspires me.

I work closely with two people who are also good friends. John Lloyd is officially my editor, he is also my mentor and counsel and gives me confidence when I am sitting at the keyboard. Eric Drewery has turned my daubs and scribbles into this lovely object. He is brilliant at keeping us on schedule and does so in the nicest possible way. Together they make this work a pleasure.

On my travels I met many people whose knowledge, comments and thoughts have informed my writings. Others have just been very kind and helpful. I thank them all for their time and patience. They are; Sue Allen, Ashdales Estate Agents, Sam Ashworth, Brian and Janet Baker, Harry Baker, Colonel James Baker, Mike Ball, Gavin Barker, Helen Beddow, Peter & Judith Blenkinsop, Rita & Peter Bunney, Barry Collis, Peter & Winifred Colven, Steve Cook, Jane Corke, Peter Crane, Alasdair Cross, Hugh Cunliffe, Bryan Curtis, Robert Cuthbert, Josh Dadd, Steve Dailly, Nick Dobbs, Rita Drewery, Charlie Durnford, Maurice Ede, Ross Flett, Joy Foubister, Robin Gordon, Duncan Grant, Terry Healey, Gill Hendry, Jon Hickling, Frank Hill & Son, Colin Hunter, Douglas Hunter, Roger Hunter, Sam Johnston, Kathleen Kemp, Mary & Charles Kennerley, Peter LeGrys, Ray Leonard, Mr & Mrs D J MacDonald, Torquil and Janice MacInnes, Mrs J MacIntosh, Annabell MacIver, Donald MacKay, George and Jane Macpherson, Andrew Maiden, Dr Jon Mills, Hilary Morcroft, Susan Morgan, Trevor Mouncey, Don Moxom, Brian Nicholson, Richard Offen, Dr Stuart Otway, Julia Peters, Debbie Podger, Prowting Homes, Herbert Ramsey, Mr & Mrs P Rance, Peter & Tan Robinson, Denis Rooney, Philip Round, Gordon Scott, Shaw, Rabson & Co, Jim (it's behind you) Smith, Heather Squires, Fulton & Susan Sweeney, John L Symonds, David Thornton, Bob and Brenda Turner, Gordon Ward, Dave Wharton, David White, Tony Wilkie-Millar, Barrie Wilkinson, Peter Wilson, Flight Sergeant E Wittaker and Geoff Wyatt.

... and also I acknowledge Peter the Seal.
(Orkney Seal Rescue)

160